C0-AQZ-981

Production Planning
and Information Systems

– Production Planning and Information Systems–

J. J. Verzijl

N.V. Philips' Gloeilampenfabrieken,
Eindhoven, Holland

A HALSTED PRESS BOOK

JOHN WILEY & SONS
New York

658.5
V 574

179254

English edition © J. J. Verzijl 1976

All rights reserved. No part of this publication may be reproduced or transmitted in any form, or by any means, without permission

First published in the United Kingdom 1976 by
The Macmillan Press Ltd

Published in the U.S.A. by Halsted Press,
a Division of John Wiley & Sons, Inc., New York

Printed in Great Britain

Library of Congress Cataloging in Publication Data

Verzijl, J   J
  Production planning and information systems.

  Translation of Plannen en informeren.
  Includes index.
  1. Production planning. 2. Management information systems. I. Title.
TS176.V47 1976   658.5'03   76–7906
ISBN 0–470–90620–0

Contents

Preface   vii

Introduction   1

1   Planning   3

2   Information   18

3   'Available capacity equals capacity in demand'   27

4   Human performance   35

5   Heuristic scheduling   37

6   Frequent 'work' mixes   42

7   Six examples of planning in a factory   58

8   Worked example of a production department   67

9   Policy information   88

Appendix: Planning factors   120

Index   123

Preface

The simultaneous production of several more or less complex commodities could not possibly be organised properly without using a great many systems competently and in proper balance, for instance systems of planning and information, estimating and post-calculation, rating, wage and salary information, work-structuring, training, career planning, co-ordination and costing. None of these is completely self-sufficient in the sense of being able to stand alone.

Planning systems can no more exist without information than fire without oxygen and are prone to fail whenever information is overdue or incomplete. Assuming that all the other systems involved are up to standard, the remedy lies in the efficient use of computers and business machines. However, since this study concerns only planning and information, the other systems will only be mentioned very briefly, as the occasion demands.

The principles and formulae on which to build systems of planning and information are shown to be no more complicated than the four 'simple' equations defining all the marvels of electricity and magnetism which are part of our daily lives and the source of all electrical equipment from electric lamps to space-craft, and from the hot-plate to the television receiver. Properly applied, these principles and formulae can go a long way towards ensuring a high standard of performance and good working conditions in any manufacturing department or factory.

Eindhoven, 1976   J. J. VERZIJL

Introduction

Planning experts will be the first to admit that theirs is an unrewarding and intricate task, aimed at keeping control over situations usually involving an enormous variety of factors, as mentioned in the Appendix. As a swimmer avoids drowning by varying his style to suit conditions, so a planner achieves results by adopting whatever method best suits the situation for which he has to plan. Planning situations range from one extreme to another; for instance, from that of a football match played at tremendous pace with new plans being evolved, and if possible thwarted, first by one side and then by the other, so that a no-score draw denotes failure of all these plans, to that of a successful attempt to beat the world record for speed skating over 10 000 metres, which simply means that the skater has managed to pace himself perfectly throughout each of the 25 circuits. Where a factory's order book is full, any enquiry from a customer as to whether a new order can be delivered by such and such a date can only be met by a skilful search for whatever tiny bit of capacity can be spared to accommodate the order conveniently, without jeopardising other delivery deadlines.

In his book *Humanity in Flux**, Pierre Bertaux defines this kind of situation succinctly in such phrases as 'Rigid planning leaves no room for manoeuvre' and 'Whoever plans, reckons without the unknown' (or 'Man proposes, but God disposes').

In industry there is really a need for a separate term to distinguish between what passes for planning, but allows new orders to be accepted regardless of risk to those already in the pipeline, and true planning in the sense of ensuring that new orders rarely (if ever) jeopardise the due completion of work taken on earlier. That is the kind of planning we shall be studying.

---

* *Mutatie van de mensheid*, in Dutch, published by Scientific Publishing Company, Amsterdam, Holland.

1 Planning

1.1 Why Plan?

Planning systems are designed to:

(1) Foster good industrial relations.
(2) Reduce production costs to a minimum.
(3) Keep throughput times as short, and amount of work in progress as small as possible.
(4) Achieve a high standard of reliability of delivery.
(5) Ensure controlled and consistent growth of productivity.

Of all the different factors which govern good industrial relations, planning and information systems are the most crucial in that they control many of the variables inherent in other systems. In fact it is true to say that none of these other factors can possibly operate effectively if the planning and information system goes wrong. Without proper planning and information it is not possible to distribute the work fairly, or at any rate as fairly as circumstances allow, amongst the work force.

This particular study will be confined to points (2), (3) and (4), and will not consider point (5) because it would involve not only a broad discussion of cost–price structure, budgeting and prices and incomes policy, but also a knowledge of just what sectors of the economy should, or should not be encouraged to develop in order to bring about 'real growth'. Our problem would then have to be placed in some kind of consistent framework, as discussed in *To Each His Own*, by J. J. Verzijl.*

1.2 How to Plan?

1.2.1 Little strokes fell great oaks

A few per cent increase in orders inevitably causes uneven ordering intervals and a variation in order quantities incompatible with the

* *Ieder het zijne,* in Dutch, published by Koninklijke Van Gorkum & Co., Assen, Holland.

need to keep stocks small and lead times short. Simple formulae confirming this statement will be demonstrated in due course, beginning with a simple planning situation of continuous production by the supplier and continuous use by the customer, and proceeding by stages to the more difficult ones involving discontinuous production coupled with more critical loading and an expanding product mix. It will be seen that even a small additional order quickly adds enormously to stocks, lead times and demand on capacity, thereby tempting customers to place excessive orders and create a vicious circle.

1.2.2 Planning situations

Planning problems involve suppliers, customers and products alike. Their governing factors are prices, material supplies, reorder dates, delivery dates and production capacity. Let us begin with a simple planning situation: suppose that a product made in one operation is to be produced in quantity by a regular supplier on behalf of a regular customer. Four different situations are then conceivable, as shown in table 1.1. We need only consider the planning problems facing the

Table 1.1

Situation	A1	A2	A3	A4
Continuous production by supplier	yes	yes	no	no
Continuous use by customer	yes	no	yes	no

supplier. There will be none, except perhaps a capacity problem, if he is able to count on *continuous* production (situations A1 and A2), since planning only presents a problem to the supplier when production is discontinuous, that is when the spare machine time has to be used to make one or more items for the same customer, or for others (situations A3 and A4). Whether a customer uses—or perhaps sells—his own products continuously or discontinuously is of no concern to the supplier.

Let us consider the planning problem arising in situation A3, i.e. discontinuous production by the supplier as against continuous production by the user. Because the investment in stock is substantial and the market 'uncertain', the customer splits his overall requirement

Table 1.2

Situation	B1	B2	B3	B4
Orders scheduled at regular intervals of so many working days	yes	yes	no	no
Same quantity ordered every time	yes	no	yes	no

into a number of order quantities, which can again be done in four different ways, as shown in table 1.2.

The outcome of situations A3 and B1 combined (regular ordering cycles and identical quantities per order) does not present a true planning problem of the kind which does arise where situations A3 and B2 coincide (orders at regular intervals of so many working days, but for varying quantities).

1.2.3 Stocks and order quantities

Example 1.1

Our first example illustrates the somewhat rudimentary planning situation of A3 and B1 combined. The customer uses 1000 items X a day whereas the supplier's daily output is 4000. Therefore the item only keeps the machine occupied for 25% of the time, during which the supplier's stock of item X builds up at the rate of $4000 - 1000 = 3000$ per day. Assuming that the customer orders 8000 every eight working days, this situation will only keep the supplier occupied for two days out of every eight. Moreover, it takes one day to set up the machine and six days to deliver the goods.

Supplier's output, customer's offtake and the combined stock level are perhaps best expressed in terms of how many days' consumption, or usage they represent. Thus, the customer of course absorbs one days' usage per day, amounting to 1000 units in the present case, whilst the supplier produces four days' usage per day, and the stock level rises at the daily rate of three days' usage. Because the frequency of orders is not necessarily cyclic, we shall refer to it in terms of the *number of days' demand*. Figure 1.1 illustrates the scheduling of orders—production, transport and usage as expressed in these terms.

The first order goes on record as soon as production begins, that is after the machine is set up. The stock of item X builds up to eight days' usage within two days, whereupon production is interrupted.

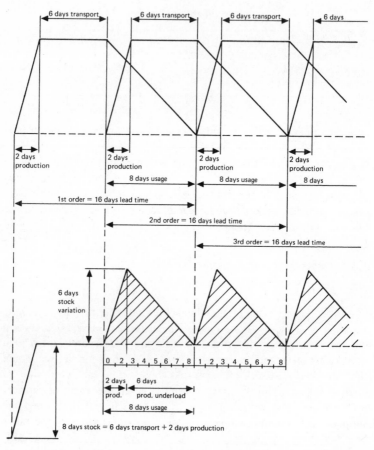

Figure 1.1 Course of stocks

Transport takes another six days, therefore usage, or perhaps sales, can commence on the ninth day and then continue for eight days in all. Because all the orders, including the first, require a lead time of 16 days, the need for continuous usage means that another batch will have to arrive on the 17th day, and go into production eight days earlier in order to provide this. Therefore, uninterrupted usage calls for the orders to run concurrently, simply because of the time it takes to produce and ship them.

Note that the base line of each triangle in the lower half of figure 1.1 spans as many days as it takes to use the 8000 units. The portion of this line on the left of the vertical spans two days, that is the supplier's production time, and that on the right of the vertical another six days which the supplier must fill as best he can with work from the same customer or from others, but at all events mainly in the interests of this regular customer. The vertical height represents the combined stock levels of supplier and customer, that is six days' usage in the present example. For all practical purposes, then, these triangles represent a situation in which transport takes no time at all and which is therefore ideal for keeping stocks as small as can be. They are very convenient for working out how stocks, production costs and risk of obsolescence are likely to be affected by increasing or reducing the batch size. The amount of stock resulting from transport time and frequency can be determined by simple addition; in the present case it is eight days' usage in all, i.e. two for production and six for transport. So much for planning situation A3, B1, in which the machine loading is dictated by the ratio of customer's usage time to supplier's production time plus set-up time.

In the present example the item only takes up 25% of the machine time, not including set-up time. The machine will have to be utilised more intensively than this to create a real planning problem. Suppose we want to start making one more item. The order for this will then have to satisfy two conditions, as follows (still referring to situation A3, B1):

(1) Allowing for set-up time, it must utilise enough of the machine time to make both items viable at prices acceptable to the customer(s).

(2) It must match the frequency of orders for item X.

To continue our example, item Y meets these conditions in that it is ordered at regular intervals of eight working days and used at the rate of 1000 items a day by the customer. Since the supplier's output is 2000 a day and $8 \times 1000 = 8000$ units are needed every eight days, it takes $8000 \div 2000 = 4$ days to produce these, with another day as set-up time. Figure 1.2 illustrates this schedule.

Example 1.2

For our second example we move from situation A3, B1 to the more fully fledged planning situation A3, B4, i.e. discontinuous production of varying quantities ordered at varying intervals. Suppose that the

Machine load

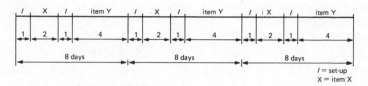

Stock variation

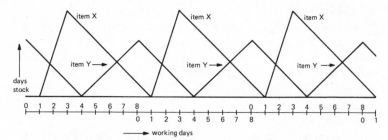

Figure 1.2   Machine utilisation and course of stocks

users, without having increased their daily usage (or sales) of items X
and Y, nevertheless begin to view the future with rather more
confidence and therefore ask for the batch size to be increased from
8000 to 12 000, or in other words from 8 to 12 days' demand. Out of
every 12 days the supplier then devotes three to producing item X
($3 \times 4000 = 12\ 000$), six to producing item Y ($6 \times 2000 = 12\ 000$) and
a day each, or two days in all, to setting up the two items, thus
completing the regular orders in 11 days, i.e. with one day's capacity
to spare. Because it would take that long to set up another item, this
spare day counts as idle time. (How that affects the cost price will not
be discussed here.)

1.2.4 Crucial formulae

It will be evident from these two examples that usage (or sales) by the
customer, production by the supplier, stock fluctuation and
customer's demand are interdependent. Given the customer's daily
usage of units, these relationships can be defined in a few simple
formulae, as follows:

$$Z = \Sigma I / (1 - \Sigma v) \tag{1.1}$$
$$V(X) = Z \times [1 - v(X)] \tag{1.2}$$
$$P(X) = Z \times v(X) \tag{1.3}$$

where Z is the demand in terms of days' usage; I is the time (days) it takes to set the machine up for the production of an item, supposing that every item made on the machine requires the same set-up time, so that $\Sigma I = n \times I$; n is the number of different items produced on a given machine during the demand period; ΣI is the total set-up time per demand period; Σv is the machine load factor stemming from all the items made in one demand period, less their set-up times; $V(X)$ is the peak stock level of item X in Z days' demand; $v(X)$ is the ratio of daily usage to daily output of item X; and $P(X)$ is the order quantity in terms of days' output of item X. (Note: these formulae are only valid where machine utilisation is 100%.)

Example 1.3

Suppose the customer manages to boost sales of item Y to 1300 a day, leaving those of item X at the original level of 1000 a day. Supplier and customer agree that the increased output must come from the same machine so as to avoid using extra tools and machines. This situation may be formulated as follows:

$v(X)$ remains at 0.25 $(1000 \div 4000)$
$v(Y)$ becomes 0.65 $(1300 \div 2000)$

So

$$\Sigma v = 0.25 + 0.65 = 0.90$$

and equations (1.1–1.3) give

$$Z = \frac{n \times I}{1 - \Sigma v} = \frac{2 \times 1}{1 - 0.9} = \frac{2}{0.1} = 20 \text{ days' demand}$$
$$V(X) = Z \times [1 - v(X)] = 20 \times (1 - 0.25) = 15 \text{ days' usage}$$
$$V(Y) = Z \times [1 - v(Y)] = 20 \times (1 - 0.65) = 7 \text{ days' usage}$$
$$P(X) = Z \times v(X) = 20 \times 0.25 = 5 \text{ days' production}$$
$$P(Y) = Z \times v(Y) = 20 \times 0.65 = 13 \text{ days' production}$$

In example 1.1 there were eight days' demand ahead with usage at the rate of 1000 items X and 1000 items Y a day, whereas now the demand period is 20 days and the daily usage 1000 items X and 1300

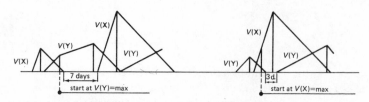

Figure 1.3   Course of stocks

items Y. In other words, the demand for both items has changed from
8 to 20 days' supply, which means that the order quantity of item X
must also be drastically increased, although usage of this item remains
unchanged. Moreover, figure 1.3 shows that the customer will run out
of item X seven days too soon if the batch increase happens to
coincide with production of item Y, or will have to wait three days for
delivery of item Y if it occurs during production of item X.

1.2.5 Formulae produce amazing results

Example 1.4

Now assume that the customer wants a third item W to go into
production on the same machine. In terms of hours the job is of little
consequence, constituting a mere 5% of the total load. However,
table 1.3 shows how much it affects the schedule. The consequences
of this insignificant rise in production are amazing in that it extends
the demand period from 20, to 60 days, while the supplier now finds

Table 1.3

Item	*v*			Demand (days)			Production (days)			Stock (days)			Price factor		
X	0.25	0.25	0.25	8	20	60	2	5	15	6	15	45	1.33	1.11	1.05
Y	0.50	0.65	0.65	8	20	60	4	13	39	4	7	21	1.33	1.11	1.05
W			0.05			60			3			57			1.05
ΣV	0.75	0.90	0.95												
	1	2	3	1	2	3	1	2	3	1	2	3	1	2	3

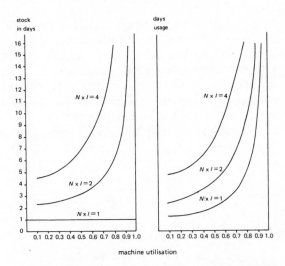

Figure 1.4 Machine utilisation against stock

that one of the items monopolises his production capacity for 15, instead of 5 days, and another for 39, instead of 13 days (three times as long). Moreover, a customer working with really minimal stock levels will initially have to wait up to 10 days for item Y, or up to 26

Table 1.4*

v	Value of Z (days)		
	$n \times I = 1$	$n \times I = 2$	$n \times I = 4$
0.2	1.25	2.5	5
0.4	1.66	3.33	6.66
0.5	2	4	8
0.6	2.5	5	10
0.8	5	10	20
0.9	10	20	40
0.95	20	40	80
0.98	50	100	200
0.99	100	200	400

* v, n, I and Z are defined on p. 9.

days for item X, depending on when the rise in production takes effect. At the same time, the respective stocks build up from 7 to 21, and from 15 to a massive 45 days' supply, drawbacks which are in no way compensated for by minor price reductions (see 1.2.6).

Figure 1.4 illustrates the interdependence of capacity utilisation, demand and inventory as exemplified in table 1.4. The chart shows how to produce successive runs of one, two and four items with Σv values of 0.8, 0.9 and 0.98 and ΣI values of one, two and four working days, respectively, on the same machine. The minor advantage of the price factor of 1.25 through 1.11 to 1.02 will eventually be balanced by rising inventory costs and added risk of obsolescence.

1.2.6 Effect on production costs

No factory can go on changing its capacity availability from day to day. For most the true situation is best described colloquially as 'being fully booked' or 'having plenty of work'. Putting the added

Table 1.5

Items X	Y	W		Number of items	Set-up time per item (days)	Set-up time (days)	Demand (days)	Max. stock in days per item	Price factor
v	v	v	Σv	n	I	$n\times I$	$Z=\dfrac{n\times I}{1-\Sigma v}$	$V(X)=Z\times(1-v(X))$	$\dfrac{1}{\Sigma v}$
0.2			0.2	1	1	1	$\dfrac{1}{0.8}=1.25$	$1.25\times0.8=1$	$\dfrac{1}{0.2}=5$
0.2	0.2		0.4	2	1	2	$\dfrac{2}{0.6}=3.33$	$3.33\times0.8=2.66$	$\dfrac{1}{0.4}=2.5$
0.2	0.2	0.2	0.6	3	1	3	$\dfrac{3}{0.4}=7.5$	$7.5\times0.8=6$	$\dfrac{1}{0.6}=1.66$

value per day at unity we find the price factor to be 1 where $\Sigma v = 1$ and 5 where $\Sigma v = 0.2$, making the production costs five times as high (see last column of table 1.5). The problem is how to optimise production costs and inventory holding costs, including risk of obsolescence. A simple example has been worked out in table 1.5.

A customer for item X whose own $v(X) = 0.2$ has for instance the following options:

(1) Keep Σv at 0.2, with one days' stock $V(X)$ in hand and a price factor of 5.
(2) Increase Σv to 0.4, with 2.66 days' stock $V(X)$ in hand and a price factor of 2.5.
(3) Increase Σv to 0.6, with six days' stock $V(X)$ in hand and a price factor of 1.66.

We must conclude that the supplier's efficiency is very much influenced by the quality of the customer's planning. The interdependence of orders from different customers has too much effect on cost to be safely ignored.

1.2.7 Stock evaluation

Let us now consider how to calculate the ideal stock level on a given day, augmented to allow for time spent on production and shipment, namely two days plus six days in the case of figure 1.1.

The inventory in terms of cash—or days' output—and that in terms of days' consumption may then be altogether different, the one being a financial criterion and the other a measure of risk of obsolescence. In both cases the truth of the assessment depends very much on its timing. Suppose for instance that we take inventory just before setting up the machine for item 1 (figure 1.5).

$$V(1) = 1$$
$$V(2) = I + P(1) + I$$
$$V(3) = I + P(1) + I + P(2) + I$$

or in general terms

$$V(n) = P(1) + P(2) + P(3) + \ldots P(n-1) + (n \times I)$$

(all in units of days)

or

$$V(n) = \sum_{i=1}^{n-1} P(i) + (n \times I)$$

In words:

> To evaluate the inventory correctly one must note when each item goes into production, how many days' demand there are and what is the ratio of daily usage to daily output (v).

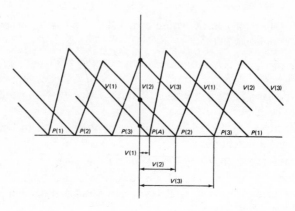

Figure 1.5 Influence of the 'count moment' on the amount of stocks

The remedy is to use a computer. Of course there is no point in taking stock on days of usage.

1.2.8 The customers

Customers fall into three categories:

(1) Occasional ones.
(2) Regular customers quite capable of doing their own planning and forecasting.
(3) Regular customers unable or unwilling to produce competent plans or forecasts.

1.2.8.1 Occasional customers

Situations involving mainly occasional customers are to be found in shops, travel agencies handling air-line reservations, or in general wherever goods are supplied from stock to the public at large. Planning is prone to present many problems, particularly for factories which merely assemble purchased items or parts and mostly have to sell from stock on the retail market, where customers are notoriously capricious. Because survival in this situation may well depend on being able to supply whatever the customer wants from stock, it is not surprising that planning systems were originally aimed at having the right items in stock at all times, and ultimately evolved into procedures for optimising inventory costs by varying batch sizes or lead times, despite the attendant drawbacks of underloading, inferior performance, relatively large working stocks and totally unrealistic delivery dates.

1.2.8.2 Regular customers with a planning system of their own

Given a product mix with only one customer for each item, the efficiency and flexibility of production control depends on the number of orders received, how many customers there are and business relations with, as well as between the customers.

1.2.8.3 Regular customers without a planning system of their own

The outcome of the third alternative is that the planning system has to stem from a policy allowing the utmost leeway (as opposed to mere fluctuation) between 'excellent service to good, regular customers submitting accurate forecasts' and 'treating all orders in exactly the same way and with equal appreciation'.

Planning policy may be based on sales, available production capacity, or both. Where there are many customers, a sales-oriented policy leads to systems aimed, as we have seen, at optimising batch sizes and inventory costs, despite the consequent problems facing the factories. On the other hand, unduly obstinate concentration on available production capacity is prone to leave the sales department with far too much stock on its hands. This study advocates neither principle individually, but instead proposes that production be sized and scheduled with both in mind. If at all possible, inevitable minor fluctuations in demand should be absorbed by adjusting the batch size accordingly.

So far it has been shown—particularly by the formulae—that planning in any situation is not a mere blueprint contrived by agreement between individuals, however well-intentioned. The same applies whatever the product mix and whatever the nature of the clientèle, and must be borne in mind when introducing any planning system if this is to be successful. Those allowing themselves to be guided by the principles outlined so far will find these equally useful in dealing with more complex planning problems.

1.2.9 The planning problem

In the planning situation defined on pp. 4–13 we are almost compelled to adopt what may be called an aggregate, or perhaps a 'theatre-booking' system of planning, whereby new orders are booked and planned to fill gaps in production, or 'idle time' in very much the same way that reserved seats are crossed off a theatre seating plan. The only difference is that whereas no more than the width of one seat is allotted to each member of the audience, regardless of girth, the 'time spans' reserved for different orders in factories vary. Factories beyond a certain size could divide their time into standard 'lengths', thereby giving the customer the option of obtaining the exact number of units he requires at extra cost by booking more than the time it takes to make them, or settling for whatever quantity can be made in the time available (figure 1.6).

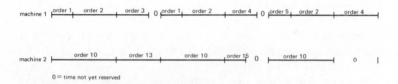

Figure 1.6   Sequence of jobs on a machine

Although factory orders which involve several jobs make it rather more difficult to analyse planning requirements, the solution to this problem is no different in principle from that of the simple examples discussed so far, whatever the sequence of operations (fixed or variable). As you will doubtless have read many times in the past 20 years—and as production managers or planners will know from bitter experience—lead times, stocks and prices have increased quickly whenever markets have hardened. At the end of the year individual productivity has (too) often increased by no more than about 5%.

Almost every page of this book therefore provides fresh evidence of how little scope planning allows and how violent is the reaction of the machinery it conceals. It follows that the only way to achieve planning efficiency, intensive loading, short lead times and flexibility is by first making a clear distinction between matters within one's control, and those beyond it, as for instance between repeat orders, constituting at least 70% of most factories' product mix, on the one hand, and new orders on the other. A new item which calls for a great deal of preliminary work should be kept out of the planning for as long as possible, so that all being well it can eventually go into production in the same way as a repeat order, albeit planned as a rush order in the first instance if necessary. To borrow another example from the world of sport, an ideal planning situation is like a game of basketball played at tremendous pace between evenly matched teams, and ending in a high-score draw simply because both sides have managed to overcome every attempt to thwart their plans.

2 Information

Jobs can be so organised that people:

(1) Do, or do not get to know one another.
(2) Receive information at random, or at agreed intervals.
(3) Say 'all there is to say', or 'as little as possible'.
(4) Prefer to stipulate 'every minor detail', or 'essentials only'.

Many of us find that good industrial, and personal relations are most likely to stem from knowing one another well and exchanging information as punctually and at as regular intervals as possible, bearing in mind just how far ahead each of us can look and without unnecessary invasion of privacy. Of course this implies the utmost delegation of authority and an organisation of parallel, rather than differently graded functions.

2.1 Giving and Receiving Information

In olden times a messenger able to bring good news from the battlefield was a very fortunate man. He got the king's most beautiful daughter—or so they say. Nowadays important letters between V.I.P.'s never go by post but instead are carried, sometimes a very long way and at great expense, by some specially appointed diplomatic emissary, who then delivers his message with due ceremony—a fairly safe as well as apparently undemanding task these days, yet one which no one would consider beneath his dignity.

Anyone with news to deliver is influential in the sense of being temporarily 'master of the situation' and therefore in charge. Moreover the recipient hardly ever assimilates the information verbatim, but instead transforms this at least into what he thinks he has heard, or should have heard in order to fit in with his own preconceived ideas. The expressions 'to be told' or 'to listen to reason' are most often used in the negative sense of 'he won't be told' or 'he won't listen to reason'. Any ex-inmate of a concentration camp can tell you that there was no better way to annoy his guards and tormentors than by doing 'exactly' as he was told. Then everything went beautifully wrong. And surely we have all heard of the general who failed to win a battle simply because his troops always followed his orders to the letter.

It is because information is so rarely assimilated without some personal touch being added that things invariably go amiss when it does happen. *We must therefore be very careful how we convey information.* Everyone, however important, in his own opinion at any rate, should realise that to others he is merely a source of information which someone else will have to work out.

2.2 Faithful Reporting

Class distinction in jobs rests mainly on position within the hierarchy, which in turn is often sustained by the power to issue, or withhold information. It follows that the particular style of management can be related to the way information is distributed amongst specific occupations. The weaker a management the longer it will delay issuing information and the more inadequate and irregular this will be. The paradox is that this kind of management is considered authoritarian, whereas in fact the more authority a management has, the more up-to-date, complete and regular is the information it passes on in a process regarded strangely enough as democratic.

2.3 Ignoring, or Getting to Know one Another

There is a brilliant French proverb to the effect that: there can be no dispute without prior agreement (*pour disputer il faut être d'accord*). To quote the eighteenth-century politician Edmund Burke: 'There can be no effective action without co-operation, no co-operation without trust, and no trust between parties not bound by common opinions, inclinations and interests.' To reach and preserve this happy state, both parties, the giver as well as the receiver of information, will have to find out in conversation just what opinions the other holds, or, where production departments are concerned, get to know and respect each other's standards. To do so the information seeker must know not only where to find his informant, but also when.

2.4 Timely or Belated Information

Next we have to decide whether information should be forthcoming at any time, or at agreed intervals. In the latter case the intervals may or may not be regular. Although the practice of issuing information 'as and when' is still widespread, the literature contains little evidence in favour of such exchanges. Despite the obvious lack of any feasible alternative in many situations, it is extremely doubtful whether they are ever really effective. Some writers do stress the importance of timing and warn that great care should be taken to avoid mutual waste of time.

2.5 Information is not a Matter of Specifying every Minor Detail

Yet another vital aspect of providing information is the object in view. Particularly in industry far too few people yet seem to recognise the importance of promptly passing on all information—whether self-acquired or imparted by others—at any rate to colleagues within relatively easy reach.

There is also a tendency to issue information in the form of 'instructions', and planners, particularly methods engineers and 'supervisors', are amongst those guilty of overdoing this. It implies lack of confidence in others, who begin to feel that they are being 'organised to death'. To quote Niels Bohr on the subject: 'The idea that we should as it were allow the individual just enough freedom to keep his deepest secrets concealed from us is beginning to obtrude.' The right to do one's work as best one can must start somewhere, as must the area within which one should be trusted to do so.

2.6 Making the Best Use of Information

2.6.1 Recognising relationships

The first essential of good planning is to make the best use of information. To do so one must be able to recognise relationships within the particular company and know how to preserve these. Of course there are many different kinds of relationship, such as:

(1) The simplest example of using one thing to find another (telephone book, name followed by telephone number).
(2) The link between two like objects on a level, for instance two drawings making up a job.
(3) The link between similar objects at different levels, for instance two components assembled into one product, which in turn goes with other components to make up another product (and so on, perhaps time after time).

(4) The relationship between two dissimilar objects, for instance a drawing and a machine both contributing to the manufacture of a product and so linked by the job.

Another element of planning is timing. Where one job is scheduled for each throughput period, the link between jobs constituting a factory order is that those in a given sequence have to be done in successive periods. In planning, dispatch decision rules govern the relationship between jobs which are part of the same factory order and, within load cycles, jobs of different factory orders but which are assigned to the same machine. It is only by recognising such relationships for what they are that one can avoid inadvertently taking on work which is bound to be at odds with other, existing relationships, or may even create new ones. New work should only be accepted if existing organisational (as well as technical) facilities are able to cope with it.

2.6.2 Recognising individual areas of activity

The kind of information one requires and even the channels through which one should receive this depend very much upon one's function within an organisation. Hence the need to recognise not only relationships, but also individual areas of activity. Perhaps the most important distinction in this connection is between:

(1) Interdependent activities in which the same means are used to achieve the same end, in which case all concerned need information on the same subjects. For example, in a production department with a hundred skilled operators at as many machines, planning covers three main areas of activity, namely order processing, production management (perhaps irreverently, but nevertheless more aptly described as 'progress chasing') and the final task performed by each of the hundred operators individually. All rules and standards will have to be defined most clearly in order to weld these people into a team.

(2) Interdependent areas of activity in which different means are used to the same end. Almost any factory has separate departments to deal with: customers, materials procurement, special tool maintenance, production, invoicing, shipping, etc. Each bears some responsibility for planning and information. Of course there are differences in complexity or degree of difficulty, as well as in the amount of money at risk.

Examples will be given later that show that planning presents the biggest problem to the production department; personnel involved in dealing with material procurement, special tool maintenance, shipping, invoicing, and, for that matter, with customers, have to submit their standards and rules of procedure to whoever is responsible for accepting orders within the production department so that this person can take these matters into account before making commitments to customers.

This sensible procedure is prone to cause friction in practice because it is regarded, quite wrongly, as a form of subjection to authority.

2.6.3 Which function carries most weight?

In practice, managements sometimes tend to attach more importance to material control than to production planning, which brings us to the well-known argument as to whether policy should be based on sales, or on production capacity. Where there are many customers for the same item, a sales-oriented policy is conducive to a system of seeking optimum batch size regardless of whether this causes the factory to be underloaded, to suffer loss of productivity or to be burdened with too large an in-process inventory. Where there is only one customer for each item, production efficiency depends entirely on what kind of order is placed, what the business relationship is like and how well the customer, as well as the producer, appreciates the problem involved. The other approach is to concentrate on available capacity. As mentioned earlier the author holds that this should at least be taken into account in deciding the volume of production.

The examples worked out in this study therefore assume production planning to be the focal point and to operate according to standards stemming from the departments responsible for materials procurement and the maintenance of special tools. Whether this is best in any given case will depend on the overall planning situation. Obviously the department liaising with customers has, should have, or at any rate should want to have a part in all of this, although (so far) custom alas dictates otherwise.

2.6.4 Block-diagram method of depicting activities

Few will deny that because novel ideas are so rare and take so long to find acceptance, most of us work in situations which can be described

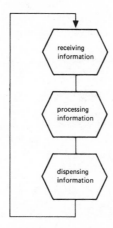

Figure 2.1 Simplified information flowchart

as 'continually recurring', and therefore analysed and presented most lucidly in the form of block diagrams (see figure 2.1). It is as well to admit that almost any job is ultimately a matter of: receiving, somehow processing and then dispensing information to someone else, who then proceeds to do the same. Take for example the simplest of activities:

B receives planned information from A, assimilates it without difficulty into a planned situation of his own and dispenses his information, planned, to C. Whatever A tells B can only count as planned information for B if he has told A what to expect of him and when, if B keeps his word to A, ... and so on.

Let us make our example a little more realistic (figure 2.2). The seeker finds the information he needs to do his job by reading from top to bottom or, where a decision is called for, from the top sideways to the left, sideways to the right, or downwards, whilst the following questions go through his mind. 'Job finished? If so, inform next in line, if not is it time to go home? No? Then are there any problems? If not I'll carry on; if so must lave it until I can get more information.'

What kind of problem-solving information the recipient is or should be entitled to memorise, or to extract from instructions, the information system, or from others must be agreed in advance and strictly adhered to by all concerned. Above all it should be

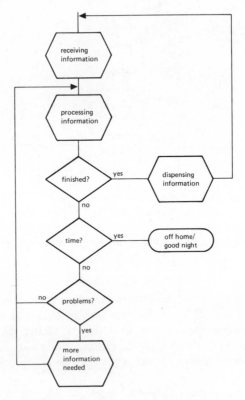

Figure 2.2 Information flowchart

remembered that whoever it is has a job to do and must dispense, or accept, whatever 'norms' are needed to do it.

Our next block diagram (figure 2.3) may be considered to be applicable to any kind of job, since apart from variations in the form of activity (operating a milling machine, handling a paint brush, writing, talking etc.) jobs differ only as regards the time they take and how systematically information is supplied before and during their implementation.

2.6.5 Workshop colloquialisms

Instead of talking about 'dispensing, or receiving information', people in workshops use more down-to-earth expressions like 'dispatching' or

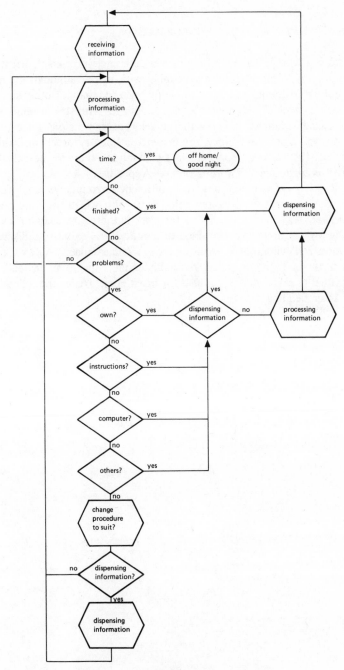

Figure 2.3   Information flowchart

'fetching work'. There is of course no difference in principle between 'coping with information' and 'coping with work', although the one seems to cost more and be more highly regarded than the other simply because most of us know a lot less about it. With this in mind, the following examples along with the relevant expressions have been borrowed from the factory, for instance a 'factory order' or 'skilled job' as the factory equivalent of what might otherwise be called a 'measured amount of information' (see Appendix).

Readers accustomed to work in different surroundings may prefer to translate these expressions into terms with which they are more familiar. Another peculiarity of factories is that, with costs in mind, they are continually constrained to aim at 100% capacity utilisation and at achieving this by ensuring that machine capacity, or available capacity as it may be called, invariably equals capacity in demand, or in other words orders scheduled for production. Hence the following chapter headings.

3 'Available capacity equals capacity in demand'

3.1 Systematic Presentation

A very simple planning situation exists when the customer's order equals the factory order, itself divisible into two or more jobs to be done in a specific sequence of operations. Production is then continuous and there are no lead-time problems, although the breakdown of the factory order into two or more operations does affect the capacity of the plant. Our aim is to ensure 100% loading by preserving a perfect balance between available capacity and capacity in demand. We begin by considering alternative process layouts for a factory order split into three different jobs. Jobs done as part of a repeated factory order may be defined as the product of capacity and process time. In the following diagrams, units of capacity are represented by lines: one man = one line, two men = two lines, three men = three lines, and so on. The stipulation that 'available capacity' equals 'capacity in demand' holds for every example throughout this chapter.

Process time, or operation time, is the term used in the factory to denote the time normally taken to do the particular job. What planners call throughput time includes the operation time to do a job and the interval between jobs belonging to the same factory order. The ratio of process time to throughput time may be very high ($1:10$ is common enough in engineering works where heuristic scheduling is in vogue). When a job happens to take as much process time as throughput time, we as planners, shall nevertheless employ the latter expression, as in the example of figure 3.1.

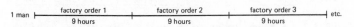

Figure 3.1 Sequence of jobs done by one man

27

According to the original work method the factory order is equivalent to the job. The next important step is to decide how to apportion the product as to 'throughput time × capacity' in order to go on utilising the capacity fully. As regards the decision to divide the throughput time into identical, or into different lengths and the capacity into equal, or into different amounts, the following permutations are possible:

(1) Identical throughput times × equal amounts of capacity.
(2) Identical throughput times × different amounts of capacity.
(3) Different throughput times × equal amounts of capacity.
(4) Different throughput times × different amounts of capacity.

Permutation (4) also offers two more alternatives:

(4a) Different discrepancies in throughput time than in capacity, or different throughput times $\overset{\neq}{\times}$ different amounts of capacity.
(4b) Same discrepancies in throughput time as in capacity, or different throughput times $\overset{=}{\times}$ different amounts of capacity.

The following simple examples show which of the five options are feasible, subject to the stipulation that 'available capacity' equals 'capacity in demand' and, of course, without any accumulation of intermediate stocks.

3.1.1 First option: identical throughput times × equal amounts of capacity

A periodic factory order taking nine hours as a single job is to be split into three jobs taking three hours each. As will be seen from figure 3.2, the factory order can be divided into jobs taking identical

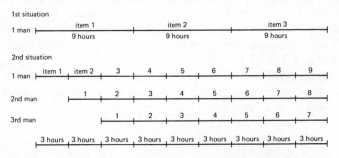

Figure 3.2   A product planned in one operation of nine hours and a product planned in three operations of three hours

throughput times (= process times) and equal amounts of capacity. How this, and all the other options cited affect capacity and in-process inventory will be discussed in section 9.2.

3.1.2 Second option: identical throughput times × different amounts of capacity

A periodic factory order taking seven man-hours as a single job is to be split into three jobs taking four hours, two hours and one hour, respectively (figure 3.3). If we choose to make the throughput times

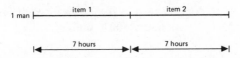

Figure 3.3 A product planned in one operation of seven hours

identical, then these will have to be at least as long as it takes to do the most time-consuming of the jobs, that is in this case four hours (figure 3.4). This means that whoever does the third job will have to complete three extra stints every four hours in order to keep fully occupied, so that three extra men will have to be employed on the first job and one extra man on the second in order to keep pace with him (figure 3.5).

'Identical throughput times × different amounts of capacity' is feasible provided that there is no objection to allowing two or more jobs of different factory orders covering seven hours to be done as three jobs taking four hours, two hours and one hour, respectively,

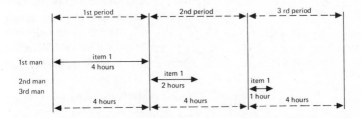

Figure 3.4 A product planned in three operations of four, two and one hours underutilised

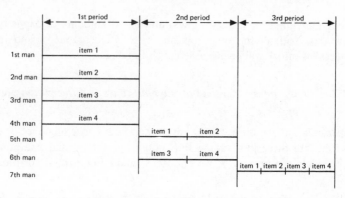

Figure 3.5   A product planned in three operations of four, two and one hours 100% utilised

during each throughput period. In effect a factory order thus spans four items at a time, in which case the throughput time for two out of three operations exceeds the process time and there can be no strict compliance with the stipulation that 'available capacity' equals 'capacity in demand' *after each item*.

3.1.3 Third option: different throughput times × equal amounts of capacity

An item produced as a factory order originally involving one job taking nine man-hours is split into two jobs taking six hours and three hours by a change of work method. Figure 3.6b shows that available capacity cannot be matched to capacity in demand per factory order, and in this case per job as well, by opting for 'different throughput times × equal amounts of capacity'. Nor is there anything to be gained by reversing the job sequence, since despite ensuring full-time employment on both the six-hour and the three-hour job, this would cause the in-process inventory of units only one third complete to accumulate progressively from job to job every six hours. Therefore the third option is ruled out if machine utilisation is to be 100%.

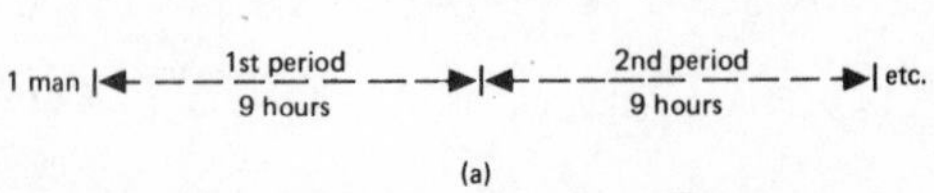

1 man |◄ — — 1st period — — ►|◄ — — 2nd period — — ►| etc.
        9 hours   9 hours

(a)

Figure 3.6a   A product planned in one operation of nine hours

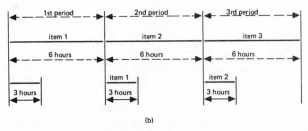

Figure 3.6b   A product planned in two operations of six and three hours

3.1.4 Fourth option: different throughput times $\overset{\neq}{\times}$ different amounts of capacity

Take for instance a factory order (the equivalent of an item) taking 22 man-hours in all, to be produced by two people working five hours each on the first, and three people working four hours each on the second operation. It will be seen from figure 3.7 that this is no more viable than the process layout calling for 'different throughput times × equal amounts of capacity'.

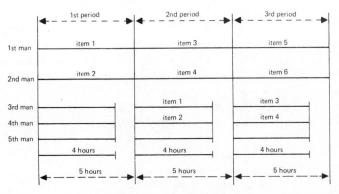

Figure 3.7   A product planned in two jobs of five hours and three jobs of four hours

3.15 Fifth option: different throughput times $\overset{=}{\times}$ different amounts of capacity

For example a factory order taking six man-hours in all and involving jobs done in three operations of duration three, two and one hours.

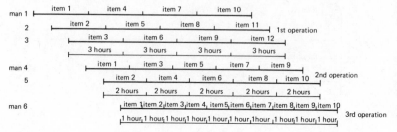

Figure 3.8   A product planned in three jobs of three hours, two jobs of two hours and one job of one hour

Now this does permit 100% capacity utilisation. Alternatively the solution could be interpreted as one of 'identical throughput times × different amounts of capacity' coupled with dispatching to individual operators, in which case the throughput time becomes six hours made up of two three-hour jobs on the first, three two-hour jobs on the second, and six one-hour jobs on the third operation. This gives the first worker three hours, the second two hours and the third, if necessary, one hour of sequencing time (figure 3.8).

3.2 How to Organise Dispatching

It follows that there are only three different methods of dispatch consistent with 100% capacity utilisation. To stress the vital importance of these three primary options as bases to which all other situations can be referred they will now be reiterated in terms of a factory order utilising capacity in the ratio of 3:2:1 and involving three operations taking six hours, four hours and three hours per job.

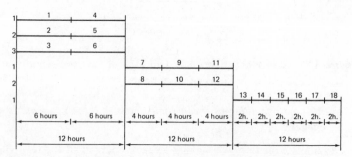

Figure 3.9   A work issue without overlapping throughput times

Figure 3.9

Prompt dispatch, without overlap, to each operation. Eighteen units in progress. The total throughput time is $3 \times 12 = 36$ hours.

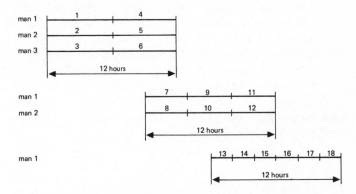

Figure 3.10 A work issue with overlapping throughput times

Figure 3.10

Simultaneous, overlapping dispatch to each operation. Fewer than 18 units in progress at any one time. Total throughput time in this case 24 hours. A gain of 33% as compared with previous method of dispatching.

Figure 3.11

Individual dispatching to operators. There are now six units at a time in progress, and the overall throughput time per unit is

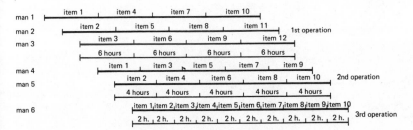

Figure 3.11 A work issue per man

$6 + 4 + 2 = 12$ hours. However, despite involving the least work in progress and throughput time per factory order, this is the most vulnerable situation of all three. [It should be noted that the fact that only these three dispatching options are consistent with 100% capacity utilisation makes it convenient for us to carry out all the relevant calculations, mainly of throughput times, minimal capacities and numbers of factory orders on hand (see section 7.1).] Hence it is essential to know after how many factory orders available capacity can be expected to match capacity in demand, at any rate in theory. Practical experience has shown that this balance can often be achieved within a very few factory orders by anyone prepared to do the arithmetic. Because such scheduling offers so many advantages, the principal methods available will be discussed in chapter 6.

4 Human performance

Human performance is recognised quite rightly as being the most important of all the factors governing production. It is a blend of speed and skill depending very much upon circumstances. We have already seen (chapter 2) that people working on the same factory order do best by:

Getting to know one another
Agreeing to finish their work and meet at prearranged intervals
Keeping one another informed
Allowing one another to get on with the job uninterrupted in the meantime.

We also saw under subsequent headings that an item, or for that matter several items, can only keep the available capacity at full stretch if the jobs involved can be broken down individually or in total into operations all taking exactly the same number of hours. With this in mind what has been described as 'heuristic scheduling' will be discussed in the next chapter. That is a blanket term for the kind of planning and information system whose characteristic features are that no one seems to know what he is likely to be doing in a few hours time, that new information may come in and have to be assimilated at any moment, that schedules are variable and that new work has to be taken on at no more than an hour's notice at most and without any prior information as to what it actually involves. Human performance can hardly be measured at all in such a situation and invariably falls well below the theoretically attainable level when evaluated by work study. The only reasonable explanation of this is that in these circumstances hardly anyone finds it possible to set himself a task which he at least, and preferably those around him, can appreciate.

Another very worrying aspect of the matter is that even where expert opinion puts the overall performance no higher than, say, 80%, the odds are against anyone reaching 85 or 90%, a fact which by suggesting that everyone is already doing the best he can is prone to get this accepted, willy-nilly, as 100% performance.

Heuristic scheduling lacks flexibility, creates long lead-times and is by no means conducive to reliable delivery schedules. Many efficiency experts advocate deliberate underloading to shorten throughput times and make the system more flexible. Yet in factories employing such scheduling no job ever works out at a performance rating of exactly 100, nor are skilled workmen ever seen to stand idle for anything from three-quarters of an hour to ten minutes (for lack of a suitable margin) between jobs and then raise the rate to 130 throughout the final half hour's work. Instead, any slack between jobs is taken up by working more slowly or abandoning the optimum work method so as to be (sometimes) short of time.

In fact the only way people can be persuaded to give their best and so make full use of plant capacity is by dispatching work to fill the same number of calendar hours every time. A great deal of useful experience with this method has been acquired since 1959. The dispatch element has been called *quantum* scheduling and is essentially a matter of giving every skilled man (meaning everyone who knows his job, regardless of training) as much work as he can normally be expected to do within a fixed calendar period, ranging from half a day to four weeks in different workshops. We found that almost all those employed in our workshops welcomed the system, which so boosted morale that productivity increased almost as a matter of course. The sole exception occurred in one of the factories where the system was first introduced, when a group of skilled toolmakers were given a quota of work to be done in one week and, unlike the other groups, did not display exactly the enthusiasm expected of them. Some weeks later, however, when the jobs involved did prove to take longer than the time stipulated, a four-week quota for teams of two was established instead, whereupon the response promptly came up to expectation.

Not the least of this system's advantages is that by restoring initiative in the use of time it creates the kind of organisation in which absence is noticed and failure to meet commitments is seen as inevitably leading to disaster.

5 Heuristic scheduling

Any form of heuristic scheduling in a factory is bound to create endless hustle and bustle in pursuit of one minor detail after another. Everyone then seems pressed for time and convinced that the factory, to say nothing of himself, is vastly overloaded. 'Inevitably so', is the managerial view, 'since there is (usually) a full year's work on the order book'. Nevertheless the accumulated down-time and the number of unscheduled hours booked to direct labour suggest rather strongly that all is not quite as cosy as it seems. No waiting time, of course—no chance of that with so much work on hand. Yet despite all this effort no one seems quite certain what tomorrow or, if on piecework, the next job will bring. Hence such frequent queries as 'How do I get hold of that?' and 'What does the thing look like?'. Any manager in that situation has to be a kind of walking encyclopaedia with a quick answer to every problem. On the other hand such answers tend to be short-lived in that they merely engender fresh questions (almost without pause). No wonder that workshops then evolve their own dispatch decision rules, somewhat at odds with those decreed by the management:

> Jobs requiring the same auxiliary tools are combined to save set-up time and so make the rate more easily.
> Tightly rated jobs and jobs involving a high percentage defective are ignored for as long as possible.
> Certain people acquire a kind of customary right to specific jobs and keep special tools aside for the purpose.
> Whatever happens to be on top of the pile is done first.

Many managers consider that the only way out of this situation is to use a computer with on-line facilities, giving this a set of rules to govern its choice of priorities.

Some of the better-known priority decision rules are:

(1) Shortest process time.
(2) First come, first served.

(3) Earliest delivery date.
(4) Factory order involving least waiting time between jobs.
(5) Earliest scheduled start.
(6) Penalty clause for late delivery.
(7) Furthest in arrears.
(8) Cumulative value (of an individual component or the order as a whole).

Of course all these rules and priority decisions have to follow a plan, which may be constructed manually or again worked out by the computer with the aid of relevant rules.

When a customer's order involves several factory orders the first step is to devise a network (figure 5.1) with the object of defining the relative timing and prospective progress of parts for a particular piece of equipment, a building, or whatever.

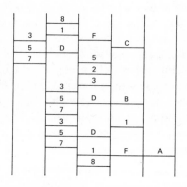

Figure 5.1 A client's order exploded into factory orders

Because capacity utilisation varies from one customer's order and one operation to another, factory managements almost always have to weave a couple of these networks together in order to load all the operations properly. To be of any real value, however, this network, essential where there are several factory orders to each customer's order, must be accompanied by a plan depicting the probable course of events. Now, delivery time less the sum of process time and probable waiting time between jobs gives us the starting date. The weak link in this calculation is probable waiting time, for which one full week's working hours less process time is taken as an average in the vast majority of factories.

According to priority decision rule (4), the average waiting time between jobs is then calculated at the outset and compared with that of all the other jobs. For instance: three working days from starting the first job to starting the second and another seven working days from finishing this to starting the next means that each job will have taken an average of five days. After all a computer is bound to do a great deal better than that. To do so it must make meticulous, last-minute decisions as to which particular job amongst so many is most certain to preserve a smooth flow of faultless work, delivered exactly on time, of course whilst keeping factory orders in progress to a minimum and making really 100% effective use of every man and machine.

To define our problem properly, however, we must now stop thinking in terms of one job/factory-order/week, because this puts too much emphasis on time per job. Instead we take elements from one job in each of eight different factory orders where each job takes five hours out of a 40-hour working week, and from one job in each of 3.5 different factory orders where each man works 35 hours a week on jobs taking 10 hours each. This works out at one job a week from each order in both cases.

Now, supposing that the computer is 'right every time', just what does it manage to do so unfailingly? At the moment of decision the computer chooses elements from a group of jobs waiting to be done. Of course this would be ideal if there was only one job to choose from, since throughput time and work in progress would then be minimal. For example, a factory order consists of three jobs to be done in a fixed sequence of operations in a workshop where there are three machines (figure 5.2).

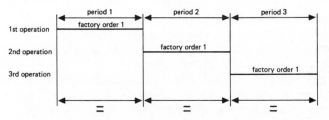

Figure 5.2 One job per throughput time available

Only one factory order per operation is in progress during each throughput time and capacity utilisation is 100%. That is only possible where each job totals the same number of working hours, in which case we do not need an on-line computer system to cope with the matter.

If the choice of elements from two jobs at a time is given, i.e. at alternate decisions, the computer is in effect choosing elements first of two jobs and then of one. Only one in the latter case because a double choice at this point would involve choosing elements from not just two jobs, but instead first from two and then from three of them, which would conflict with the stipulation of one job in every two as throughput time (figure 5.3).

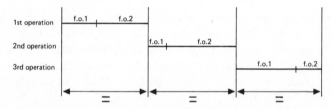

Figure 5.3　Two jobs per throughput time available

The situation resembles the previous one in that it can only exist where every two jobs done total the same amount of time, which can be arranged by pairing off jobs beforehand to have the same throughput time, another task which does not require the services of an on-line computer system—not even when it takes a throughput time for instance five times the sequencing period to achieve a balance of 'available capacity' equal to 'capacity in demand'. The rules for achieving this are merely a matter of sequencing factory orders in groups of five so that the five jobs take approximately the same amount of time in each sequencing period (figure 5.4). It makes no difference whether these factory orders are, or are not in a fixed sequence or how much the job times vary.

The obvious conclusion is that we can do without an on-line system wherever there is only 'one job' to choose elements from at a time. Given a wider choice from, for instance, up to five jobs at a time, there will be one fewer to choose from on each successive occasion down to

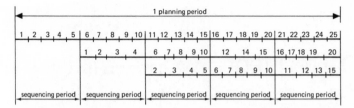

Figure 5.4 Four or five jobs per throughput time available

zero, whereupon, of course, another batch of up to five jobs will have to be progressed. That being so, it is very much more sensible and economical to give as much advance notice of all five jobs as possible. Should the last job scheduled have to be switched to first position several times in a row, that might perhaps be thought enough to warrant on-line reporting but for the fact that it would land us right in the middle of our first schedule (figure 5.2), and to be 'right every time' in that situation would be a miracle indeed.

Another drawback of heuristic scheduling is that the variation in batch size and in re-order and delivery dates virtually rules out the spot checks on current or retrospective rise and fall of orders, accurate at least within plus or minus 2%, which are needed to ensure a reliable lead time and to keep control over inventory and capacity (see section 1.2.5).

6 Frequent 'work' mixes

6.1 Two Items Constituting a Factory Order

A factory makes two items in two operations performed in the same sequence time after time; dispatch is without overlap. Item X takes four man-hours, three of them spent on the first, and the other one on the second operation, and item Y the same, but this time with one man-hour devoted to the first, and the other three to the second

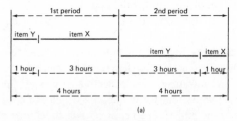

Figure 6.1a Two products form one factory order of two operations; issue not overlapped

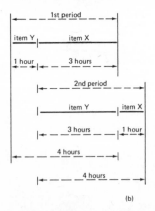

Figure 6.1b Two products form one factory order of two operations; issue overlapped

42

operation. The two items are combined into one factory order involving two four-hour jobs consistent with 'identical throughput times × equal amounts of capacity' and the advantages this offers, namely that capacity, represented by two operators (plus machines), orders in progress and throughput time per operation, are all minimal (figure 6.1a). However, proper sequencing does permit some overlap (figure 6.1b).

6.2 Two Items Routed Separately

Two items are dispatched without overlap as separate jobs done in the same sequence of operations time after time. As in the previous example both items X and Y take four man-hours in all, three for the first and one for the second operation in the one case and the opposite way round in the other. Because these items are routed separately as individual factory orders, however, the consequences are as follows:

Route A: three operators and as many machines on first operation; one operator and machine on second operation.
Route B: one operator and machine on first operation; three operators and as many machines on second operation.

To be fully loaded, both routes require at least four operators and as many machines, making eight of each in all (figure 6.2). This is in many ways inferior to the previous solution (section 6.1).

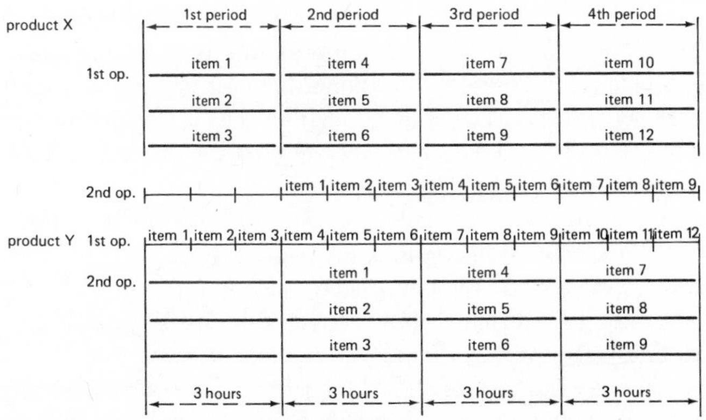

Figure 6.2   Two products manufactured in two separate production lines

Conversely, the following example illustrates the advantages of routing. The relationships involved can be analysed more conveniently by adopting the notation employed in section 9.2, thus:

lowest common multiple (LCM) of 7, 4 and 2 is 28
highest common factor (HCF) of 7, 4 and 2 is 1.

With two items X and Y in parallel production we have the situation given in table 6.1. The throughput time per operation is 28 hours. There are 28 jobs in progress per operation. The capacity is at least $7 + 4 + 2 = 13$ men. This makes $3 \times 28 = 84$ jobs in progress overall, each as part of a different item, so that in effect there are also 84 items in progress at the time. Given dispatch without overlap the throughput time is 84 hours.

Table 6.1

	1st operation (man-hours)	2nd operation (man-hours)	3rd operation (man-hours)
Item X	4	2	1
Item Y	3	2	1
Together	7	4	2

Now, dividing the factory into two product groups, one for each item, reduces work in progress and throughput time without requiring any more than the minimum capacity of $(4 + 2 + 1) + (3 + 2 + 1) = 13$ men (+ as many machines). Item X has four as its LCM and one as its HCF, making four hours of throughput time per job and four units in progress per operation. Overall throughput time is thus reduced from the original 84, to 12 hours and work in progress on item X from 42 $(84 \div 2 = 42)$ to 12 units. The corresponding figures for item Y are six hours of throughput time, and six units of work in progress, per operation and 18 in all, or in other words its throughput time is reduced from 84 to 18 hours and work in progress from 42 $(84 \div 2 = 42)$ to 18 units. (Of course this work could also be progressed with overlap, which would take less throughput time overall, but no less per operation and leave just as much work in progress.) It should also be noted that a factory may well be making tens of items paired to take exactly as many hours per operation every time.

6.3 Several Factory Orders Together Constituting one Day's Work for each Skilled Man

As in the previous example the sequence of operations is fixed and work is dispatched without overlap. We shall see that three times the amount of work to be dispatched (that is less than the lead time required by the customer) is consistent with the stipulation that 'available capacity' equals 'capacity in demand'.

Our next example makes no distinction between a customer's order and a factory order. Each factory order, then, is divided into three jobs totalling three operations, performed in a fixed sequence. One man and one machine are assigned to each operation. All at once a regular pattern begins to emerge.

To make available capacity equal capacity in demand three conditions must be satisfied, as follows:

(1) The hours per operation must be in the same 1 : 1 : 1 ratio as the hours worked by the operators.
(2) Enough work to fill three man-hours must be ordered on average every hour.
(3) These two conditions must be fulfilled within a given period, time after time.

A situation of this kind will now be presented in more detail. At a given moment there are eight factory orders waiting to go into production as shown in table 6.2.

Table 6.2

| Factory order no. | Duration of operation (hours) | | |
	Op. 1	Op. 2	Op. 3
8	3	6	4
7	5	0	5
6	2	5	3
5	4	2	4
4	3	4	2
3	2	1	5
2	1	4	1
1	4	2	0
	24	24	24

The hours spent on each operation must be in the ratio of $1:1:1$. We want to dispatch eight hours', that is exactly one day's work on each operation and seek to do so by trial and error as follows. Combining orders 1 and 2 we find:

$$4:2:0$$
$$1:4:1$$

$$5:6:1$$

and then seek another order, whose first operation takes three hours. Order 8 looks promising, but on adding this to the previous total we obtain

$$5:\ 6:1$$
$$3:\ 6:4$$

$$8:12:5$$

therefore 1, 2 and 8 together will not do. We then drop order 2 and try orders 1 and 3, thus obtaining:

$$4:2:0$$
$$2:1:5$$

$$6:3:5$$

and then seek an order whose first operation takes two hours, that is order 6:

$$6:3:5$$
$$2:5:3$$

$$8:8:8$$

These three orders combine to make the right ratios and so go into the factory as one. Although, as you may suspect, this example has been worked out beforehand, it is nonetheless true that the method has been employed successfully on a great many occasions and is very much easier than perhaps it appears. Moreover in reality the hours can often be varied to some extent thanks to the co-operation of others doing their best to make the system work. Had the work been dispatched on the principle of first come, first served, then the successive ratios would have been as shown in table 6.3.

Table 6.3

	Op. 1		Op. 2		Op. 3
After order 1	4	:	2	:	0
After order 1 + 2	5	:	6	:	1
After order 1 + 2 + 3	7	:	7	:	6
After order 1 + 2 + 3 + 4 and so on	10	:	11	:	8

Although it is difficult to work out exactly how much influence this has upon throughput time, and therefore upon 'idle time' of men and machines, it is bound to affect waiting times and work in progress very severely.

6.4 Several Factory Orders Together Constituting one Throughput Period of Work for each Skilled Man. Dispatched with Overlap. Fixed Sequence of Operations. Some Minor Variation in Hours per Job

Each factory order involves three jobs to be done in a fixed sequence of operations. Six factory orders consistent with 100% loading are selected from the order book, as shown in table 6.4. Without overlap the throughput time of these six orders would be too long; the question is how to obtain the optimum overlap? With this in view only one priority rule is correct: Dispatch whichever job has the shortest initial operation first, add an hour or so for the second operation, make the third the longest and try to preserve the same ratio between

Table 6.4

Factory order no.	Op. 1	Op. 2	Op. 3
1	2	3	4
2	4	2	3
3	3	3	3
4	3	2	4
5	2	4	2
6	4	4	2
	18	18	18

Table 6.5

Factory order no.	Op. 1	Op. 2	Op. 3	Cumulative ratios				
1	2	3	4	2	:	3	:	4
4	3	2	4	5	:	5	:	8
3	3	3	3	8	:	8	:	11
6	4	4	2	12	:	12	:	13
5	2	4	2	14	:	16	:	15
2	4	2	3	18	:	18	:	18

the hours per operation as these accumulate. As it happens this means beginning with factory order 1 in our example and proceeding in what then emerges as the optimum sequence 4, 3, 6, 5, 2 (see table 6.5). It will be seen from the cumulative ratios columns that the increment persists up to the first operation of factory order 5, but that the second job time of this order is one hour longer than of the third operation for the same order. The remedy is to time the transport between jobs to compensate this discrepancy (figures 6.3 and 6.4). The sequence is governed by the apportionment of hours for each factory order. Any

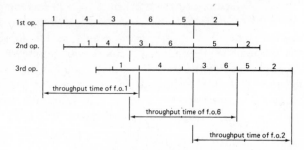

Figure 6.3   Overlapped throughput times without transit times

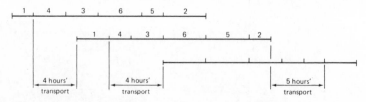

Figure 6.4   Overlapped throughput times with transit times

other dispatch decision rule is bound to result in fewer jobs/factory order/period. Given enough transport time we can even ignore the cumulative increase in hours per operation.

6.5 Several Factory Orders Together Constituting one Throughput Period of Work for each Skilled Man. Dispatched with Overlap. Fixed Sequence of Operations. Substantial Variation in Hours per Job

The example shown in table 6.6 involves the familiar approach of sequencing in order of more hours per operation. Table 6.7 gives the optimum solution.

Table 6.6

Factory order no.	Duration of operation (hours)			
	Op. 1	Op. 2	Op. 3	Op. 4
1	1	3	1	1
2	1	3	1	1
3	5	1	3	1
4	1	1	4	2
5	1	1	0	2
6	1	1	0	0
7	1	1	1	0
8	1	1	1	5
9	1	1	1	1
10	1	1	2	1
	14	14	14	14

Note that the number of hours per operation for factory order 2 drops (between the second and third operations) in the 'Cumulative ratios' column of table 6.7, a fact to be given due consideration in connection with the timing of transport: with four hours for transport from job to job of the first factory order (8), there is but one three-hour transport period involved here (figure 6.5).

Should the remedy of sequencing in order of more hours prove inadequate then the only alternative is to so extend the sequencing period to allow time for each man to complete several jobs. That has

Table 6.7

Initial sequence	Factory order	Hours per factory order	Cumulative ratios			
1	8	1 1 1 5	1 :	1 :	1 :	5
2	4	1 1 4 2	2 :	2 :	5 :	7
3	5	1 1 0 2	3 :	3 :	5 :	9
4	9	1 1 1 1	4 :	4 :	6 :	10
5	10	1 1 2 1	5 :	5 :	8 :	11
6	1	1 3 1 1	6 :	8 :	9 :	12
7	2	1 3 1 1	7 :	11 :	10 :	13
8	3	5 1 3 1	12 :	12 :	13 :	14
9	7	1 1 1 0	13 :	13 :	14 :	14
10	6	1 1 0 0	14 :	14 :	14 :	14

been done in figure 6.6, where the 'route' (or machine line) is composed of seven operators at as many machines completing the first operation six times in each sequencing period, as well as 12 jobs/man/period on the second, and 24 jobs/man/period on the third

Figure 6.5 Overlapped throughput times with transit times

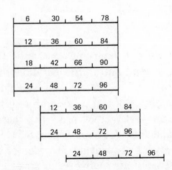

Figure 6.6 Throughput times per 6, 12 and 24 jobs overlapped

operation. Sequencing traces the 'ribbon' of initial operations from job 1 to job 96, clipping it into 16 six-job 'lengths' to be completed in each successive sequencing period. The actual throughput time per operation thus spans four, and the total throughput time per factory order three sequencing periods.

Although the principle of 'different throughput times × different amounts of capacity' might well be applied here and is in fact better in theory, practical experience has shown that limiting the sequence break-points to three instead of seven creates so much more team-spirit in the sense of 'knowing what to do and improvising for instance during momentary absences' and 'coping with rejects to be reworked in the same period' that the solution illustrated in figure 6.6 must be considered far superior in the present case.

The same remedy can also be applied in another way, that is leaving the sequence of the groups of six initial operations to be performed periodically by each man from job 1 to job 96 in abeyance, so as to perhaps save set-up time and preserve some margin for error in process planning. Figure 6.6 shows that one in six initial-operation jobs for one of six factory orders is complete in one sequencing period by the product group employing capacity in the ratio of 4 : 2 : 1, whilst 'available' equals 'in demand' at regular intervals of four sequencing periods. Job-time for the first operation averages seven hours. If necessary the relevant number of jobs/men/sequencing period for the other operations can be calculated as well as the average job-time for these, yielding information which helps the order processor to work faster.

Remember that the jobs leading into successive throughput periods may work out at odd periods of more than an hour, in which case the transport time between jobs will have to be amplified slightly to allow for the consequences of varying throughput times (see section 6.7).

6.6 Several Factory Orders Together Constituting one Throughput Period of Work for each Skilled Man. Dispatched with Overlap. No Specific Sequence of Operations. Substantial Variation in Hours per Job

Just as any factory order is bound to contain more of some operations than of others, so some factory orders are bound to involve the most common sequence of operations. Moreover neither the relevant figures nor the average hours per job are prone to any other than gradual (if at all perceptible) change. Thanks to these facts a range of items, some of whose factory orders have no specific sequence of operations, presents less of a problem than might otherwise be the case. As always a balance of 'available capacity' equals 'capacity in demand' is achieved after spending a given number of calendar hours on each operation.

To simplify matters let us suppose that each factory order involves four operations, and that capacity equivalent to one operator and machine is employed on each of these. Available capacity then equals capacity in demand at intervals of 14 hours. The range in the present example covers 10 factory orders and the most common sequence of operations is 1, 2, 3, 4. The actual sequences per factory order are listed in table 6.8. The different sequences of operations are spread

Table 6.8*

Factory order no.	Sequence of ops.	Hours/job
1	1 2 3 4	1 3 1 1
2	3 1 2 4	1 1 3 1
3	2 1 3 4	1 5 3 1
4	1 2 3 4	1 1 4 2
5	1 2 3 4	1 1 0 2
6	2 1 4 3	1 1 0 0
7	1 2 3 4	1 1 1 0
8	4 1 2 3	5 1 1 1
9	1 2 3 4	1 1 1 1
10	3 4 2 1	2 1 1 1

* See also table 6.6.

out across one or more extra columns, that is four at most where the factory orders involve that number of operations and one of the sequences is 4, 3, 2, 1, not included in the present case. Distribution across three extra columns is preferred in this case because it has been stipulated:

That the operation throughput times are to be identical.
That dispatch is to be organised with overlap.
That we want to dispatch all the factory orders in the same throughput period despite the varying sequences of operations.

Table 6.9

Factory order no.	Op. sequence	Column 1	Column 2	Column 3
1	1 2 3 4	1 2 3 4	0 0 0 0	0 0 0 0
2	3 1 2 4	0 0 3 0	1 2 0 4	0 0 0 0
3	2 1 3 4	0 2 0 0	1 0 3 4	0 0 0 0
4	1 2 3 4	1 2 3 4	0 0 0 0	0 0 0 0
5	1 2 3 4	1 2 3 4	0 0 0 0	0 0 0 0
6	2 1 4 3	0 2 0 0	1 0 0 4	0 0 3 0
7	1 2 3 4	1 2 3 4	0 0 0 0	0 0 0 0
8	4 1 2 3	0 0 0 4	1 2 3 0	0 0 0 0
9	1 2 3 4	1 2 3 4	0 0 0 0	0 0 0 0
10	3 4 2 1	0 0 3 4	0 2 0 0	1 0 0 0

As shown in table 6.9, factory orders 1, 4, 5, 7 and 9 follow the most prevalent sequence of operations. Factory order 2 begins at operation 3, implying that the 'prior' operations 1 and 2 take zero time. Because operation 4 does not follow operation 3, it is also given a nought in column 1. Factory order 3 also skips the first operation initially, another nought, and puts this in place of operation 3, making two more noughts, whilst factory order 6, treated in the same way, likewise produces 0 2 0 0 in the first column. Factory order 8 has three noughts followed by operation 4 as the first job. Factory order 10 has two noughts followed by operations 3 and 4.

Then proceeding to column 2 we find that factory order 1 involves no work done and therefore has four noughts. Now factory order 2 has the first operation in second place, following upon the third already accommodated in column 1, with the fourth operation last in line. Factory order 3 has a nought instead of the second operation, whilst the other three fall neatly into place. That brings us to factory order 6 in which the first and fourth operations fall into place in column 2, leaving the third operation to go in the last column. Factory order 7 is wholly accommodated in column 1, likewise factory order 9. At this stage the three remaining operations of factory order 8 are also in the proper sequence. Factory order 10 transposed to column 2 leaves one operation to go in the last column.

Next, the hours per job can be entered in columns 1, 2 and 3 (see table 6.10), as in the corresponding column of table 6.8. The sequence per 14-hour throughput period is then as follows. First comes the factory order whose hours per operation, in ascending order, show the

Table 6.10

Factory order no.	Column 1	Column 2	Column 3	Total
1	1 3 1 1	0 0 0 0	0 0 0 0	1 3 1 1
2	0 0 1 0	1 3 0 1	0 0 0 0	1 3 1 1
3	0 1 0 0	5 0 3 1	0 0 0 0	5 1 3 1
4	1 1 4 2	0 0 0 0	0 0 0 0	1 1 4 2
5	1 1 0 2	0 0 0 0	0 0 0 0	1 1 0 2
6	0 1 0 0	1 0 0 0	0 0 0 0	1 1 0 0
7	1 1 1 0	0 0 0 0	0 0 0 0	1 1 1 0
8	0 0 0 5	1 1 1 0	0 0 0 0	1 1 1 5
9	1 1 1 1	0 0 0 0	0 0 0 0	1 1 1 1
10	0 0 2 1	0 1 0 0	1 0 0 0	1 1 2 1
Totals	5 9 10 12	8 5 4 2	1 0 0 0	14 14 14 14

most difference. That happens to be factory order 8, with 2 as the next, and so on as shown in table 6.11.

Since the 'cumulative' column invariably shows more hours assigned to the fourth, than to the third operation, more to the third than to the second and more to this than to the first, dispatch presents no problems. Now switching to column 2, factory orders 1, 4, 5, 7 and 9 have already been sequenced, leaving the situation shown in table 6.12. Plotted for full overlap, the result is shown in figure 6.7.

Ignoring transport time between jobs, dispatch problems emerge in two places, namely as between the third and fourth operations of

Table 6.11

Factory order no.	Hours per order	Cumulative hours
8	0 0 0 5	0 0 0 5
2	0 0 1 0	0 0 1 5
10	0 0 2 1	0 0 3 6
3	0 1 0 0	0 1 3 6
9	1 1 1 1	1 2 4 7
7	1 1 1 0	2 3 5 7
5	1 1 0 2	3 4 5 9
4	1 1 4 2	4 5 9 11
6	0 1 0 0	4 6 9 11
1	1 3 1 1	5 9 10 12

Table 6.12

Factory order no.	Hours per order				Cumulative hours			
	0	0	0	0	5	9	10	12
10	0	1	0	0	5	10	10	12
3	5	0	3	1	10	10	13	13
2	1	3	0	1	11	13	13	14
8	1	1	1	0	12	14	14	14
6	1	0	0	0	13	14	14	14

Only factory order 10 is then represented in column 3.

Column 3

Factory order no. 10	1	0	0	0	14	14	14	14

factory order 3 and from the second to the third operation of factory order 8. That being so we must be careful about introducing for instance some four hours of transport time, as will be seen from figure 6.8. Factory order 8 then runs into difficulty on no less than two occasions, whilst factory order 2 comes to grief between operations 3 and 2. Yet assuming that transport between jobs takes

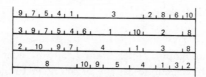

Figure 6.7   Fully overlapped throughput times

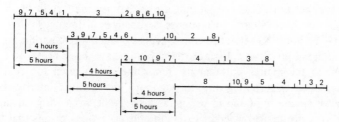

Figure 6.8   Overlapped throughput times with four hours' transit time

no time at all thanks to an extremely competent truck operator, a
solution is still to hand (see figure 6.9).

By and large, the efficacy of this solution depends upon:

The variation in the number of hours per job.
How much the sequence of operations varies.
The labour relations.

Experience has shown that a great many snags can be overcome by
keeping the process planners informed as to the consequences of non-
compliance with the stipulated sequence of operations and number of

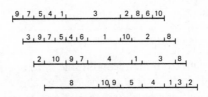

Figure 6.9   Correct overlapped throughput times

jobs per factory order. Also that operators within a group are prone
to display the utmost ingenuity when faced with the challenge inherent
in working to 'time horizons'.

6.7 Varying Throughput Times Soon Lead to Underloading and/or Increasing Intermediate Stocks of Work in Progress

As demonstrated earlier the only way to ensure 100% capacity
utilisation coupled with overall vision is by planning for identical
throughput times. Yet for all that it may happen that the throughput
time has to be altered in response to changes in factory orders or
work methods. Not that the consequences of such an alteration are at
all difficult to assess. In fact there would have been no reason to
mention the matter but that its importance is so often too readily
overlooked. Shortening the throughput time creates intermediate
stocks which are bound to persist as long as the work force sustains
100% performance, whereas extending the operations means that the
difference in throughput time will have to be accepted as idle time in
every operation but the first.

6.8 Transport is a Job between Jobs

The tendency to pay (too) little attention to transport between jobs is all the more regrettable because this is not only as much of a task in itself as any other, but can even be considered paramount in that it occurs as often as all the other jobs combined. Inter-job transport tasks in a factory employing 400 people to do 10 jobs/person/week total no less than 4000, i.e. 24 000 minutes = 400 hours, or 10 man-weeks at 6 minutes, or as much as 25 man-weeks at 15 minutes per task.

Throughput time per transport task is of course of the utmost importance. Whereas efficient organisation can reduce it to a matter of minutes, throughput periods of several days are no exception where bad organisation leads to factory orders going astray. One reason for potential (or actual) disorganisation of this kind in factories employing 'skilled' labour is that the wage system classes truck operators as 'unskilled', although one competent man on a truck can work 'miracles' by exercising a very great deal of influence upon stocks of work in progress as well as on the total complement of truck operators required.

7 Six examples of planning in a factory

Although our explanation of factory planning in theory can now be made more realistic than hitherto by introducing such activities as invoicing and so forth, we had best continue to think in terms of a simple planning situation for reasons which will soon be apparent. Suppose that:

> Supplier and customer maintain the same throughput-time, namely 40 hours.
> Individual job times vary so little about an eight-hour average that any five jobs selected at random are bound to constitute 40 hours of work.
> The capacity allocator is expert enough to get exactly 40 hours of work at a time out of each machine.
> Nothing unforeseen occurs.

Now, despite bringing the problem well within our grasp in terms of simple arithmetic, these assumptions still leave us face to face with the most difficult aspect of planning, that is how to avoid biting off more than one can chew. With this in mind six possible cases will now be exemplified.

Example 7.1

Each item (= product) is ordered by one customer only. Each item is made from 'in-house' material with 'in-house' tools as one job on a

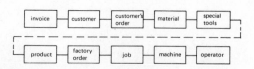

Figure 7.1   Main operations of a client's order

58

machine. An invoice is issued for each customer's order. An order for one item is completed in each cycle, and that order constitutes a full machine-load. The operator must be given a specific task to perform in each planning period. Invoices must be issued for each item in each planning period. All demands can then be met by combining these data per item per cycle, or merely per cycle.

Example 7.2

Each item is ordered, together with several others, by one customer. All the items are made of the same material, always available, there is no planning problem or need for special tools, therefore neither these nor the material need be specified. Each customer's order calls for an invoice. Each item constitutes a single job, and about 20% full load, for a machine. Each operator tends one machine.

In figure 7.3, we now set about combining all those activities whose interrelationships do not present a problem. The relationship between

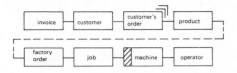

Figure 7.2 Relationship between the operations of a client's order

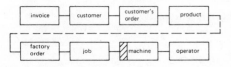

Figure 7.3 Relationship between the operations of a client's order

order and machine is a job within a given planning cycle. We therefore want to know what customer's orders to assign to each operator, i.e. to each machine, in a planning period. To solve that problem we must find out what jobs are to be done on each machine in each cycle.

Whoever accepts the orders needs to know what time has already been allocated and when there is still some to spare, which means

Figure 7.4   Relationship between job and machine

keeping a record of jobs already assigned to each machine for *n* periods ahead, with gaps to accommodate new work coming in (see for instance figure 1.6).

Example 7.3

The only difference between this and example 7.2 is that invoices are now restricted to one per customer in each planning period. The relationship is simplified as shown in figure 7.6. Now the invoicing department must be told what jobs for each customer are to be completed (and shipped) in each period.

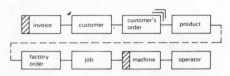

Figure 7.5   Relationship between the operations of a client's order

Figure 7.6   Relationship between invoice, job and machine

Example 7.4

In the present example (see figure 7.7) each customer's order is invoiced and there is only one customer for each item. Each customer's order is for a single item and equivalent to the relevant

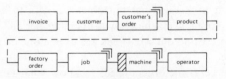

Figure 7.7   Relationship between the operations of a client's order

factory order completed in three operations on three machines, each of which has to do five jobs for as many factory orders in a given period. The question is which of the machines will do these jobs in period 'n', seeing that the next jobs for the same factory orders will then have to be completed in period '$n+1$' and the last of them in period '$n+2$'? The machine–job relationship is the same as in example 7.3 (again assuming that job times vary very little about an eight-hour average).

The order administrator keeps a record of all incoming factory orders arranged as to throughput time and period, whilst the same basic data can be used to prepare similar lists under headings of throughput time and operator.

Example 7.5

A customer places a 'customer's order' for several assemblies of various items none of which occurs more than once in any assembly. Each item constitutes a factory order for three jobs in a fixed sequence of operations (see figure 7.8). Figure 7.9 shows the relative time schedule of items, assemblies and customer's order for one such

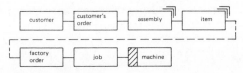

Figure 7.8 Relationship between the operations of a client's order

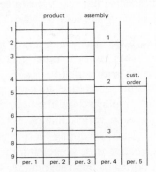

Figure 7.9 Explosion of a client's order

order, where a single job for each factory order is completed every sequencing period (counting assembly of the items as a job in itself). Not that this is ever likely to happen in practice owing to certain facts of life which must be learned in order to plan properly. For instance:

> What about the relations between customers? Do they appreciate the need for co-operation?
> How will that affect order administration?

Most sizeable factories nowadays employ more than one order administrator, perhaps one for each of a few major customers, or for every two or three of several 'smaller' ones. Obviously these officials will have to work to rules compatible with proper planning. That

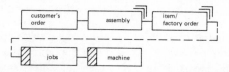

Figure 7.10   Relationship between the operations of a client's order

being so, our 'network' of relationships can be simplified as shown in figure 7.10. This calls for the following information:

> What jobs are to be done, on which machine and in what period?
> What items are to be made up, into which assemblies, when and by whom?
> Which assemblies constitute each customer's order, in what period are they to be made and by whom?

It follows that far from being planned to adjust itself automatically, every assembly plant needs its own order administrator to apply appropriate dispatch rules and establish feasible norms.

Despite there being no difference in principle between order acceptance procedures employed by the assembly plant and its components supplier, it is to their common advantage that one of them take charge of each incoming customer's order, namely whichever happens to receive this, whereupon the other is bound to comply with whatever norms its opposite number sees fit to establish.

The worked example presented in the next chapter illustrates the similar case that departments responsible for material procurement and special tool maintenance have to submit to norms imposed by the production department. Norms of the kind an assembly department might be expected to impose on its components supplier are:

That enough acceptable items for x subassemblies be produced in each throughput-period.
That these x subassemblies be sufficient for y assemblies.
That the components for these assemblies be delivered no later than two sequencing periods after they are due.

Example 7.6

Let us conclude with a worst-case example of customer's orders at many different levels, involving anything from two or three, to a vast number of drawings apiece, factory orders ranging from one, to fifty or more jobs without any fixed sequence of operations, a great deal of variation in hours per job, several items almost impossible to make, with numerous requests for in-process modifications from the customer, and a work force plagued by most inopportune illnesses and requests for time off, to say nothing of a very high rate of labour turnover. Yet given real determination to cope with this horrible situation, we can still continue to see our way clear by adopting the following approach to the problem (figure 7.11).

By insisting that one job for each factory order be done during every throughput period, instead of trying to combine identical items for the same, or different customers into one bulk factory order (for instance because this would save very little set-up time) we manage the following time 'explosion' (figure 7.12). The capacity allocator takes appropriate action wherever identical items 'happen' to have

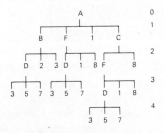

Figure 7.11 A timeless explosion of a client's order

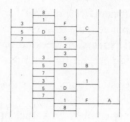

Figure 7.12   A planned explosion of a client's order

been scheduled for the same period. The main difference between this and example 7.5 is that the production schedules of components and subassemblies are interwoven. This calls for prompt and specific information based on norms accepted by all. (Of course the third of the assembly norms imposed on the components supplier in our previous example cannot apply in this situation.) Given a proper choice of throughput time, planned underloading during each such period and avoidance of undue overlap, matters really work out surprisingly well.

To sum up, all planning and information systems are similar in principle to the one illustrated in figure 7.13. The kind of relationship needed depends partly on the planning factors and above all upon the size and complexity of customers' orders, whilst the scope of relationships throughout the system is governed by the form of production control adopted (heuristic scheduling or some other alternative).

The more common planning rules, which an order administrator can apply in any situation, are:

Accept only as many factory orders per throughput period as the factory can complete in that time. *That is the most important rule of all.*
Schedule one job for each factory order in each throughput period.

Also note that the order administrator may very well be compelled to modify his plans time after time and allow for half-promises in respect of new orders, without making that an excuse for altering sequencing or throughput times, or changing the norms without notice. (Although the term 'throughput period' is used exclusively throughout this book, 'planning period' is equally appropriate, or perhaps more so in some

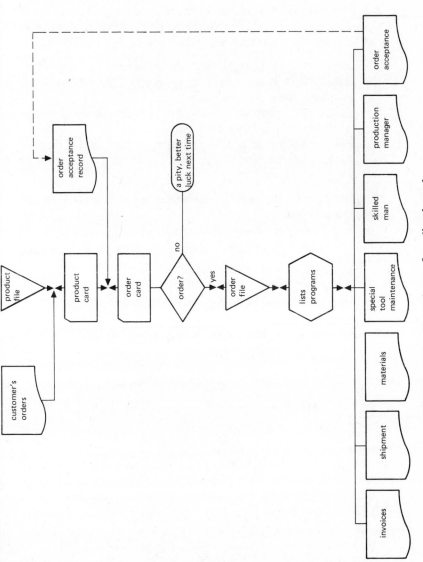

Figure 7.13 Flowchart of a client's order

situations.) Moreover it is the order administrator, rather than the capacity allocator and the skilled operators, who has to absorb most of the pressure exerted on the company by customers.

Some dispatch rules invariably needed by production management and capacity allocator alike are that:

> Substitutes for those off sick should always be obtained by transferring people from amply manned, to undermanned machine groups without delay.
>
> Skilled men temporarily short of work should be transferred to wherever there is work for them.
>
> Failure to complete a job for a factory order involving many of these should be remedied at once by resorting to overtime or staggered working hours.

Information for the order administrator must cover at least one throughput period.

Essential rules for briefing operators:

> Information concerning the next throughput period should be issued as soon as possible, together with assurance that all the preliminary work has been done.
>
> Operators should be briefed individually when working on their own, but in groups when working on 'shared' items, in which case group members should be allowed the utmost discretion as to the division of labour.

8 Worked example of a production department

8.1 Customers' Orders and Job Sizes

Suppose that a production department makes some 1500 different items a year, 80% of them ordered by one, 13% by two, 3.5% by three and less than 0.5% by more than 3 of 40 different customers (therefore there are no deliveries from stock). 90% of these items are made in a single operation, 5.5% in two, and the remaining 0.5% in three operations. 28% of the customers are regulars, planning as best they can. Now, the total run is divided into order quantities, ordered at regular intervals. Table 8.1 shows just how far this strategy pays off.

The results confirm that business relations are excellent, as implied by the acronym EGGCLIK (Each Good or Genuine Client is King) used for the branch of our planning system handling such relationships, as a token that any dependable customer can safely depend on us to supply him. Theatre-booking scheduling is used in the factory to give the utmost assurance that agreed quantities will be delivered on the agreed date (see section 1.2.9).

Through knowing exactly which of the items on repeat order present least of a problem in production, the order administrator is able to guarantee their quantity, whilst avoiding any commitment other than as to the time that will be spent on more troublesome items. The customers, aware of the need for this, raise no objections.

The consequences upon our strategy (worked out for a group of 14 machines) are as follows. Items reordered at fixed intervals are divided into groups designated monthly, bimonthly, quarterly, four-monthly, biannually and annually. Monthly items are easiest to plan in that, unlike those of the other groups, they do not have to be fitted in with any other item. For instance a bimonthly item must be co-ordinated with one other, a quarterly one with two others, and so on. It is particularly necessary to know the reorder interval of an item when this is to be superseded.

Plans *invariably* cover 180 hours at a time (that being necessary in the EGGCLIK system to minimise work in progress and to know the exact quantity used by the customer in each planning period). Job size

Table 8.1

Deviation from 'forecast' quantity (%)	As % of total number of orders
± 0– 10	40
±10– 30	25
±30– 60	25
±60–100	10

Quantity ordered per year	Forecast (%)	True (%)
1	22	18
2	16	22
3	20	14
4	10	10
6	18	16
12	14	20

Note: This rather rudimentary example has been chosen because it would take a book in itself to work out a really elaborate one on the mere off-chance that it might happen to reflect a situation familiar to many readers.

is expressed as a ratio v and change-over times average a fairly consistent 3.6 hours. Down-time per item per order is known, as are the spoilage and the delivery conditions applicable to each customer. The order administrator plans the time per factory order to include these down-times and spoilage. 427 orders for the next 12 planning periods, grouped according to the EGGCLIK system, have already been received (see tables 8.2–8.7).

Table 8.2

No. of orders	× v	Monthly Factory order no(s).	v
2	0.02	101 and 102	0.04
1	0.04	103	0.04
2	0.05	104 and 105	0.10
2	0.08	106 and 107	0.16
1	0.09	108	0.09
1	0.13	109	0.13
3	0.15	110, 111 and 112	0.45
1	0.23	113	0.23
1	0.37	114	0.37
			$\Sigma v = 1.61$

14 items are to be made $14 \times 12 = 168$ times

Table 8.3

No. of orders	× v	Bimonthly Factory order no.	v
1	0.01	201	0.01
1	0.02	202	0.02
2	0.03	203 and 204	0.06
1	0.04	205	0.04
1	0.06	206	0.06
2	0.07	207 and 208	0.14
1	0.09	209	0.09
1	0.18	210	0.18
1	0.25	211	0.25
1	0.29	212	0.29
			$\Sigma v = 1.04$

12 items make $12 \times 6 = 72$ factory orders.

A ratio v of 0.04 assigned to an item means $2 \times 0.04 = 0.08$ months of work on that individual item every 2 months.

Table 8.4

No. of orders	Quarterly $\times v$	Factory order no.	v
1	0.01	301	0.01
1	0.17	302	0.17
1	0.55	303	0.55
			$\Sigma v = 0.73$

3 items make $3 \times 4 = 12$ factory orders.
A ratio v of 0.55 means $3 \times 0.55 = 1.65$ months of work on that item every 3 months.

Table 8.5

No. of orders	Four-monthly $\times v$	Factory order no.	v
4	0.01	401–404	0.04
2	0.05	405 and 406	0.10
1	0.06	407	0.06
1	0.07	408	0.07
4	0.08	409–412	0.32
1	0.11	413	0.11
1	0.14	414	0.14
1	0.15	415	0.15
1	0.17	416	0.17
1	0.27	417	0.27
1	0.29	418	0.29
1	0.35	419	0.35
1	0.66	420	0.66
			$\Sigma v = 2.73$

20 items make $20 \times 3 = 60$ factory orders.
A ratio v of 0.66 means $4 \times 0.66 = 2.64$ months of work on the particular item every 4 months.

Table 8.6

No. of orders	Biannually × v	Factory order no.	v
1	0.01	601–611	0.11
7	0.02	612–618	0.14
2	0.03	619 and 620	0.06
3	0.04	621, 622, 623	0.12
3	0.05	624, 625, 626	0.15
4	0.06	627–630	0.14
2	0.07	631 and 632	0.14
3	0.10	633, 634, 635	0.30
2	0.11	636 and 637	0.22
1	0.15	638	0.15
1	0.26	639	0.26
1	0.37	640	0.37
1	0.70	641	0.70
1	0.83	642	0.83

$\Sigma v = 3.79$

42 items make 84 factory orders.
A ratio v of 0.83 means $6 \times 0.83 = 4.98$ months of work on one item every 6 months.

Table 8.7

No. of orders	Annually × v	Factory order no.	v
20	0.01	701–720	0.20
5	0.02	721–725	0.10
1	0.03	726	0.03
1	0.04	727	0.04
1	0.06	728	0.06
1	0.09	729	0.09
1	0.16	730	0.16
1	0.90	731	0.90

$\Sigma v = 1.58$

31 items make 31 orders.
A ratio v of 0.9×12 makes 10.8 consecutive months of work on one machine.

The number of hours left over for production depends on the number of change-overs in each planning period, as shown in table 8.8.

Table 8.8

n = number of change-overs per planning period	Leaving Σv
1	0.98
2	0.96
3	0.93
4	0.91
5	0.89
6	0.87
7	0.84
8	0.82
9	0.80
10	0.78

8.2 Capacity Utilisation

8.2.1 Monthly group

There are 14 items with a $\Sigma v = 1.61$ (table 8.9). More than one, but probably not more than two machines are required. According to table 8.8, $n = 7$ leaves a Σv of 0.84, that is 1.68 with two machines, which is more than 1.61, so that these will suffice.

Table 8.9

Machine 1		Machine 2	
Factory order no.	v	Factory order no.	v
114	0.37	113	0.23
112	0.15	111	0.15
101	0.02	110	0.15
108	0.09	109	0.13
107	0.08	106	0.08
105	0.05	104	0.05
103	0.04	102	0.02
	$\Sigma v = 0.80$		$\Sigma v = 0.81$

8.2.2 Bimonthly group

Here we have 12 items with $v = 1.04$, which calls for more than one machine (see table 8.10). This leaves machine 2 with $0.87 - 0.44 = 0.43$ to spare in the first month, and with nothing to do in the second.

Table 8.10

	Machine 1		
Month 1		Month 2	
Factory order no.	v	Factory order no.	v
212	0.58	211	0.50
210	0.36	209	0.18
		208	0.14
		205	0.08
	$\Sigma v = 0.94$		$\Sigma v = 0.90$

Note: The load ratio v for each bimonthly item is twice that stipulated in the table for items made from month to month.

	Machine 2	
Month 1		Month 2
Factory order no.	v	
207	0.14	
206	0.12	
204	0.06	(not yet scheduled)
203	0.06	
202	0.04	
201	0.02	
	$\Sigma v = 0.44$	

8.2.3 Quarterly group

There is just one item whose quarterly load ratio, that is the original v multiplied by three, proves greater than unity. The first month in the cycle of three is fully occupied. There is 0.27 to spare in the second, and 0.46 in the third month (see table 8.11).

Table 8.11

	Machine 1				
Month 1		Month 2		Month 3	
Factory order no.	v	Factory order no.	v	Factory order no.	v
303	0.98	303	0.67	302	0.51
		301	0.03		

8.2.4 Four-monthly group

Four items (417 to 420 inclusive) (table 8.12) have a four-monthly, or four times the monthly, load ratio v greater than unity, showing that each constitutes more than a month's work for one machine.

Table 8.12

	Machine 1						
Month 1		Month 2		Month 3		Month 4	
Factory order no.	v	Factory order no.	v	Factory order no.	v	Factory order no.	v
420	0.98	420	1	420	0.66	418	0.85
				418	0.31		etc.
							0.12
							to spare
		Machine 2					
419	0.98	419	0.42	417	0.98	417	0.10
		414	0.56			415	0.60
						407	0.24
		$\Sigma v = 0.98$				$\Sigma v = 0.94$	
		Machine 3					
416	0.68	413	0.44	410	0.32	405	0.20
408	0.28	412	0.32	409	0.32		
		404	0.04	406	0.20		
		403	0.04	401	0.04		
		402	0.04				0.77
							to spare
	$\Sigma v = 0.96$		$\Sigma v = 0.88$		$\Sigma v = 0.88$		$\Sigma v = 0.20$

8.2.5 Biannual group

Load ratio v multiplied by six for the biannual group leaves just an odd factory order 80% loaded throughout the six months. It seems a good idea to reserve one machine until this order is completed. All being well the sixth month will be available for other items. Factory order nos. 641, 640 and 639 then come next in order of size (table 8.13). $\Sigma v = 0.13$, which is less than 0.5 and can therefore be absorbed in spare time from other groups.

8.2.6 Annual group

Ratio v multiplied by 12 reveals that factory order nos. 731, 730 and 729 take more than a month on a machine. Factory order nos. 731 and 729 can be scheduled properly on one machine (table 8.14).

8.2.7 Summary

Allowing for 20 hours delay and 3.6 hours of change-over time per item in each planning period, and with due regard to orders already accepted and scheduled, 14 machines will have to be held in readiness, namely:

Two for the monthly group
Two for the bimonthly group
One for the quarterly group
Three for the four-monthly group
Four for the biannual group
Two for the annual group.

This leaves the following machine times to spare:

Period (months)	2	2	4	6	6	12
Spare time (months)	1	0.5	0.75	0.5	0.25	3.5

Thus, the total unscheduled capacity is 1.3 machines.

Note that the 80–20 rule again applies in that 5 items (4% of the total) account for 32%, 9 items (8% of total) for 23%, and a further 15 (or 12% of total) for 18% of the capacity available. That leaves the remaining 27% distributed amongst another 93 items (76% of the total).

Table 8.13

Machine 1

Month 1		Month 2		Month 3		Month 4		Month 5		Month 6	
Factory order no.	v	Factory order no.	v	Factory order no.	v	Factory order no.	v	Factory order no.	v	Factory order no.	v
641	0.98	641	1	641	1	641	1	641	0.22	638	0.90
								632	0.66	610	0.06
								611	0.06		
								$\Sigma v = 0.94$		$\Sigma v = 0.96$	

Machine 2

Month 1		Month 2		Month 3		Month 4		Month 5		Month 6	
640	0.98	640	1	640	0.24	639	0.83	636	0.66	635	0.60
				639	0.74	618	0.12	626	0.30	630	0.36
				$\Sigma v = 0.98$		$\Sigma v = 0.95$		$\Sigma v = 0.96$		$\Sigma v = 0.96$	

Machine 3

Order	v	Order	v	Order	v	Order	v	Order	v	Order	v
634	0.60	633	0.60	631	0.42	726	0.36	622	0.24	615	0.12
629	0.36	628	0.36	632	0.42	625	0.30	621	0.24	614	0.12
				610	0.06	623	0.24	616	0.12	613	0.12
								609	0.06	612	0.12
								608	0.06	605	0.06
								607	0.06	604	0.06
								606	0.06	603	0.06
										602	0.06
										601	0.06
$\Sigma v = 0.96$		$\Sigma v = 0.96$		$\Sigma v = 0.90$		$\Sigma v = 0.90$		$\Sigma v = 0.84$		$\Sigma v = 0.78$	

Backlog

Factory order nos.	v/month	v/6 months
617	0.02	0.12
619	0.03	0.18
620	0.03	0.18
624	0.05	0.30

Table 8.14

Machine 1

	Month 1		Month 2		Month 3		Month 4		Month 5		Month 6	
	Factory order no.	v	Factory order no.	v	Factory order no.	v	Factory order no.	v	Factory order no.	v	Factory order no.	v
	731	0.98	731	1	731	1	731	1	731	1	731	1

	Month 7		Month 8		Month 9		Month 10		Month 11		Month 12	
	Factory order no.	v	Factory order no.	v	Factory order no.	v	Factory order no.	v	Factory order no.	v	Factory order no.	v
	731	1	731	1	731	1	731	1	731	0.82	729	0.92
									729	0.16		

Machine 2

	Month 1		Month 2		Month 3		Month 4		Month 5		Month 6	
	Factory order no.	v	Factory order no.	v	Factory order no.	v	Factory order no.	v	Factory order no.	v	Factory order no.	v
	730	0.98	730	0.94	728	0.72	727	0.48	726	0.36	725	0.24
							701	0.12	709	0.12	716	0.12
											708	0.12

	Month 7		Month 8		Month 9		Month 10		Month 11		Month 12	
	Factory order no.	v	Factory order no.	v	Factory order no.	v	Factory order no.	v	Factory order no.	v	Factory order no.	v
	724	0.24	723	0.24	722	0.24	721	0.24	720	0.12	719	0.12
	715	0.12	714	0.12	713	0.12	712	0.12	718	0.12	717	0.12
	707	0.12	706	0.12	705	0.12	704	0.12	710	0.12	710	0.12
									703	0.12	702	0.12

8.3 Organisation

Everyone in the departments responsible for material procurement, special tool maintenance, shipping and invoicing is aware that planning presents most of a problem to the production department and they must therefore help as best they can by accepting whatever norms it sees fit to impose, in preference to their own. Within the production department, liaison with customers is delegated to an order administrator, whose planning activities are acknowledged to be the most difficult of all by production management and operators so that these, in turn, accept the norms he imposes. Accordingly, matters are organised as follows.

8.3.1 The operators

Each operator needs the following information to perform his task competently and with a minimum of supervision:

Which are the machines in his care?
What items are to be made on each machine and, where relevant, in what sequence?

Also the following particulars of each item:

Die or mould number and material number
Set-up time, cycle time, percentage defective and idle hours
Delivery batch size, guaranteed or otherwise
Delivery conditions as to acceptance of deviations from quantity ordered.

He in turn dispenses the following norms:

To the materials supplier:

Percentage defective per item.

To the diemaker:

Immediate reports of failures as and when they occur
Reports of any 'suspicious' noises considered significant
Time required for next job after each repair.

Information already supplied to the order administrator:

His monthly output
Whether or not willing to work more than normal overtime

When taking time off/holiday
Whether percentage defective has been fairly estimated
Whether probable delay has been fairly estimated
Rate acceptable
Product good or bad.

Each operator is also asked to:

Endorse the sequence of good and bad jobs
Report any jobs that prove too easy
Seek assistance with, and above all report any jobs that go
badly wrong.

The work sheet issued to each operator once per planning period is based for the most part on his own norms and very largely reflects information originally supplied by him (see table 8.15).

8.3.2 The order administrator

The order administrator needs two kinds of list to do his work properly. First, a list of all the orders already accepted for processing on each machine, giving the total hours to be spent on them in the next 12 months (see table 8.16). Another list for each regular customer, specifying all the orders scheduled for the next 12 months, which enables him to negotiate with the customer should orders build up, or run down unduly (see table 8.17).

8.3.3 The production manager

The production manager is able to plan efficiently with the aid of the same information supplied to the order administrator, and obtain any further details he may need from the operator's work sheet. Given the operators' norms and those obtained by work study, together with his own knowledge of items which are, or are not prone to give trouble, he has no difficulty in adjusting capacity accordingly.

8.3.4 The customers

Because an integral planning and information system is designed to enlighten, rather than to deliberately mystify customers, the larger of these are already being supplied with information on the progress of

Table 8.15

Machine	Factory order no.	Tool	Material	Set-up time	Total time	% rejects	Delivery conditions	Guarantee	Quantity	Customer	Remarks
Mr. R. Jones Calendar norm 180					Machine Group 17 20 hours delay				Month of September Average set-up time 3.6 periods at a time		
11	114	10668	11	36	230	2	1	qty	15000	C.I.F.A.	
	112	11170	11	36	200	2	1	qty	20000	K.I.P.	
	101	10969	11	36	260	1	1	qty	30000	C.F.M.	
	108	10274	17	32	170	3	2	qty	4000	Tom	
	107	10470	17	38	290	2	2	qty	7000	Dick	
	105	10670	22	40	100	2	7	time	10000	Harry	
	103	10466	22	34	360	4	7	time	18000	Smith	
22	212	27769	34	36	940	1	1	qty	8000	K.I.P.	
	210	21870	17	40	660	2	1	qty	12000	Adm.	

Table 8.16

Machine		Sept.	Oct.	Nov.	Dec.	Jan.	Feb.	Mar.	Apr.	May	June	July
					Schedule as of September							
17.11		114 23	114 23	114 23	114 23	114 23	114 12					
		112 20	112 20	112 20	112 20	112 24						
		101 26	101 26	101 26	101 26							
		108 17	108 17	108 17	108 17	108 17						
		107 29	107 29	107 29	107 29	107 29						
		105 10	105 10	105 10	105 10							
		103 36										
17.22		212 94		212 94		212 94		212 94				
		210 66		210 66		210 66	210 66	210 66				

Table 8.17

List of orders per customer

Factory order no.	Reorder interval*	This month	Oct.	Nov.	Dec.	Jan.	Feb.	Mar.	Apr.	May	June	July	Aug.	Sept.	Customer 3		
															Machine group	Op.	Shift
114	1	37000	37000	37000	37000	37000	39000	39000	39000	40000	40000	stop	stop		043	1	1
106	1	4000	4000	4000	4000	4000	5000	5000	5000	6000	6000	6000	7000	7000	043	2	1
207	22		6000		6000		6000		6000		6666		6666		043	1	1
414	42		118000			118000			118000						032	2	1
412	42		3200				2200					4000			043	1	1
631	63	2100						2100						2800	043	3	1
618	64		4800						7200						043	2	1
616	65			4800						4800					043	3	1
605	66				2000						2000				043	3	1
721	75	72000									70000				043	2	1
	77												72000		043	2	1

* 1 = monthly
2 = bimonthly
6 = biannual
7 = annual
65 = every six months in the fifth month
63 = every six months in the third month

goods they have ordered. Admittedly this is merely a modest approach to what should eventually be a register of 'information for different customers', giving particulars of any items on order that have to be made on a type of machine of which only two or three are available.

8.3.5 Material procurement

To perform his task properly, the materials buyer must know:

> The exact quantities of specific materials needed on each machine (together with the names of individual operators and where to find each machine) (see table 8.18)
> The supplier and any prospective alternative suppliers of each material
> Delivery time and order quantity
> Reorder frequency and dates of all the items made.

All these particulars are kept in a card file in the materials procurement department. The materials buyer recognises the list of authorised materials as his version of the 'schedule of orders accepted', which may only be altered according to norms for lead time and spoilage per material with effect from two months ahead. The present example postulates long-term contracts with suppliers of a relatively few materials ordered at two-monthly intervals, with only minor variations in usage between orders. As before, everyone is asked to endorse beforehand whatever task they will then be expected to perform.

8.3.6 Repair and maintenance, special tools department

The man in charge of special tools needs to know what tools will be needed on which machines, and when (see table 8.19). He in turn is required to:

> Tell the operator how long any minor faults will take to repair, in terms of throughput-time instead of hours per repair
> Do his utmost to avoid down-time (by staying in close touch with the operator responsible for 'his' dies, and noting the number of units obtained from each die and whether the probable deadline for overhaul, or perhaps die-replacement, has been reached).

Table 8.18

Materials as of September

Material	Machine	Factory code	Sept.	Oct.	Nov.	Dec.	Jan.	Feb.	Mar.	Apr.	May	June	July	Aug.	Customer
11	17.11	114	20	20	20	20	20	10							C.I.F.A.
11	17.11	112	25	25	25	25	30								K.I.P.
11	17.11	101	30	30	30										C.F.M.
11	18.13	180	80	80	80	80	80	80	80	80	80	80			H.L.M.
11	19.15	181	18	18	18	18	18	18	18						H.E.F.A.
12	19.45	419		80				80				80			Tom
12	21.66	621	100						100						Dick
12	22.37	370			60			60			60				Harry
17	17.11	108	100	100	100	100									C.O.R.
17	17.11	107	80	80	80	80									Dick
17	17.22	210	120	60	120	60	120		120	60					Tom
17	19.15	160	60	60	60	60	60	60							H.E.F.A.
22	17.11	105	50	50	50										Smith
22	17.11	103	50												Harry
34	17.22	212	90	90	90		90		90						K.I.P.

Table 8.19

Tool	Machine	Overhaul limit	Up to Sept.	Oct.	Nov.	Dec.	Jan.	Feb.	Mar.	Apr.	May	June	July	Aug.	Factory order no.
						Tools as of September									
10668	17.11	300	120	14	16	17	19	20	21						114
11170		400	100	40	42	44	46	49							112
10969		1200	200	63	66	19									101
10271		400	80	11	11	12	12								108
10490		180	80	18	19	19	20								107
10670		150	80	20	21	22									105
10466		800	200	220											103

What the die maker needs to know about each die is:

Who designed it
The grade of steel
The maker/supplier
The heat treatment
Date ordered and when received
Total run, year and order quantity
Probable date and quantity of new dies
Code number
Customer
Machine on which die is to be used.

The die shop keeps all these data up to date together with the number of units made in a written card file, copied where necessary once a month from the individual die records.

The members of the special tools department responsible for maintenance rarely make the tools themselves, but are accountable for the delivery of new dies. Hence they have established the following norms:

Orders for up to five new dies a week subject to at least eight months' lead time will be passed without question

Those with less than five months' lead time are invariably subject to discussion, whereby the final decision rests with the die maker.

Special tools are given code numbers whose:

First digit may be 1, 2, 3, 4, 5, 6 or 7, depending on the cycle of production (1 denotes a monthly item, 2 a bimonthly one, and so on). For incidental customers the first digit is an 8 if they are dependable and a 9 if they are not

Second and third digits range from 01 to 12 depending on the month, whilst the fourth and fifth denote the year of origin of the particular tool. For instance a tool used every month and completed in June 1969 will be coded 10669.

Sets of two or three tools completed for items in the same reorder group during the first nine months of the year merely involve adding the second digit to the code numbers so as to make these for instance 10669, 11669, 12669, 13669 and 14669 in respect of June 1969. Those completed in months 10, 11 and 12 are back-dated to September from October to mid-November and brought forward to the following January after that time.

9 Policy information

9.1 General

Ultimately, information is needed where performance is in doubt. For instance there may be evidence of malfunction strong enough to suggest a possible cause, yet evoking the need for a wider range of data to explore in search of inspiration, without giving any really definite idea of what to look for, or where to look. In other words this poses a question which cannot be answered without collecting the necessary information. If it is worth asking, the question is bound to be original, in which case it will almost certainly call for information not available in the required form (ready availability of information implies that the question itself is suspect and should very often be withdrawn altogether). For example, there may be a query as to:

> Which is our best customer?
> Which of our customers are we—unintentionally—mishandling?
> Does our order book warrant rearranging our plant?
> Should lead times be cut down, and if so, how?
> Which special-tool supplier is best for which items?
> Should capacity be extended, and if so, to which machine?

Often the questioner himself is still somewhat uncertain what it is he wants to know. He needs time to think about it as well as an 'output' of information to 'play about with', in an attempt to define relationships, find patterns and establish guidelines in the three distinct phases of progress towards understanding and decision.

With the data to hand we begin to ponder the situation, which involves unearthing 'tentative lines of enquiry' from a mass of facts not at all in the order in which we need them to answer our question. 'Doubts' have to be expressed in terms of matters affecting the principles or structure of the organisation.

Each of the following sections suggests some way of re-examining, and perhaps improving the organisation of production.

9.2 Effect of Number of Jobs and Hours per Job for each Factory Order upon Throughput Times, Work in Progress and Capacity Devoted to each Operation, with a View to 100% Capacity Utilisation

Some simple formulae for calculating the effect of operation loading upon minimal capacity, shortest throughput time and number of factory orders in progress in cases of dispatch with, and without overlap will now be exemplified.

9.2.1 Minimum of capacity

Example 9.1

A factory order involves three four-hour jobs, making 12 hours of process time in all. What are the least capacity and throughput time needed for dispatch without overlap and how many factory orders are in progress? In figure 9.1 the minimum capacity is plotted.

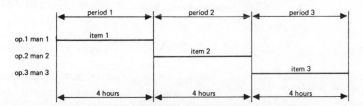

Figure 9.1   Production line for factory orders in three jobs of four hours each

Conclusion:

> This calls for three operators each working on one of three operations, naturally for different factory orders
> Throughput time per job is four hours
> Throughput time per factory order is 12 hours
> Rate of completion at least one factory order every four hours.

Example 9.2

A factory order involves two four-hour jobs and one two-hour job, making 10 hours of process time in all. As will be seen from figure 9.2:

The minimum capacity is $2 + 2 + 1 = 5$ operators

Throughput time per job is four hours

Throughput time per factory order is 12 hours

Minimum rate of completion: two factory orders every four hours

There are two jobs per operation, and therefore a total of six factory orders in progress at all times.

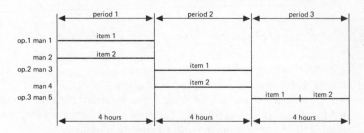

Figure 9.2 **Production line for factory orders in three jobs of four, four and two hours**

Example 9.3

A factory order involves a three-hour, a two-hour, and a one-hour job, making six hours of process time in all. A certain amount of juggling (figure 9.3) produces the right answer.

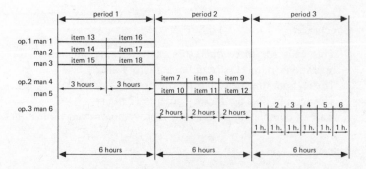

Figure 9.3 **Production line for factory orders in three jobs of three, two and one hour**

Conclusions:

The minimum capacity is $3 + 2 + 1 = 6$ operators
There are six factory orders in progress during each of the three operations making 18 factory orders in all
Throughput time per job is six hours
Throughput time per factory order is 18 hours
Minimum completion rate: six orders every six hours.

Formulae for calculating minimum capacity, the associated throughput times and the number of factory orders in progress (where dispatch is without overlap) are easily deduced from these examples.

9.2.2 Least capacity calculation

$$\text{Least capacity} = \frac{\text{factory order, in hours}}{\text{HCF* of operation times}} \text{ in terms of manpower.}$$

The least capacity figure for the examples just given are:

Example 9.1: $12/4 = 3$ operators
Example 9.2: $10/2 = 5$ operators
Example 9.3: $6/1 = 6$ operators

9.2.3 Throughput time per operation

Throughput time $TT = LCM\dagger$ of hours per operation. Thus, the TT figures are:

Example 9.1: 4 hours
Example 9.2: 4 hours
Example 9.3: 6 hours

The throughput time per factory order (for work scheduled without overlap) is the LCM of hours per operation, times the number of operations. $TT = LCM \times n$, in hours.

9.2.4 Number of factory orders in progress

$$FOIP = \frac{\text{LCM of hours per operation}}{\text{HCF of hours per operation}} \times \text{number of operations.}$$

* HCF = highest common factor
† LCM = lowest common multiple

FOIP figures are thus:

> Example 9.1: 4/4 × 3 =   3 orders
> Example 9.2: 4/2 × 3 =   6 orders
> Example 9.3: 6/1 × 3 = 18 orders

Now another example to illustrate the effects of favourable, and adverse ratios of this kind upon the whole course of events. A factory order involves three operations taking nine hours, another nine, and three hours, respectively, or 21 hours in all. An improved work method now shortens the first operation from nine, to eight, and the factory order to 20 hours.

It emerges from the formulae that originally:

> Min. capacity = 21/3 = 7 operators
> FOIP = 9/3 × 3 = 9 orders
> TT = 9 × 3 = 27 hours

Whereas following the improvement:

> Min. capacity = 20/1 = 20 operators
> FOIP = 72/1 × 3 = 216 orders
> TT = 72 × 3 = 216 hours

Because a mere 5% gain in process time can prove so very expensive in terms of capacity, throughput time and in-process inventory, it will doubtless be evident that work cannot be planned and organised really efficiently without paying due regard to a great many different factors concurrently.

9.2.5 *Work in progress*

Work in progress is almost impossible to define unambiguously because it has more than one aspect. From the point of view of a customer placing an order, this will remain 'in progress' until delivered to him. The supplier's situation is altogether different in that he usually has to have material either readily available, or in stock from the outset. Work is then done on the material, and paid for more or less as soon as completed, whereas the supplier does not get his money back until some months after delivering. He is only really concerned with ways and means of completing and delivering the factory order as quickly as possible and at least cost and therefore must do his utmost to limit the train of operations and select optimal ratios, or in others words the optimal HCF and LCM, so that from his point of view work in progress can be counted in terms of factory orders and man-hours.

9.2.6 Work in progress in terms of factory orders

Accordingly, our aim is to have as few factory orders as possible running concurrently, and to do so we must ascertain how many such orders there are in the following situations:

Identical throughput times × equal (or different) amounts of capacity without overlap in dispatch.

$$\text{FOIP} = \frac{\text{LCM}}{\text{HCF}} \times n$$ in terms of factory orders, thus giving the following:

Example 9.1: $4/4 \times 3 = $ 3 factory orders
Example 9.2: $4/2 \times 3 = $ 6 factory orders
Example 9.3: $6/1 \times 3 = 18$ factory orders

Different throughput times $\overline{\times}$ different amounts of capacity with overlap in dispatch.

In that case there are quite simply as many factory orders in progress as people employed on them (figure 9.4).

9.2.7 Work in progress in terms of man-hours, with overlap in dispatch

Formulated in words:

FOIP = Σ cap. in op. × (cap. in op. + cap. in previous operations)

Take for example a recurrent factory order involving a three-hour, a two-hour and a one-hour job and so taking six hours in all (figure 9.4). Our count refers to the vertical line, at a time when jobs for factory

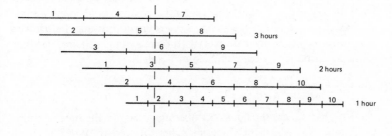

Figure 9.4 Minimum amount of work in progress

orders 7, 5, 6, 3, 4 and 2 are in progress. The following figures refer to jobs completed plus those in progress:

Factory order no.	Hours
2	$1 + 2 + 3 = 6$
4	$2 + 3 = 5$
3	$2 + 3 = 5$
6	$3 = 3$
5	$3 = 3$
7	$3 = 3$
Total	25

Or formulated as Σ cap. in op. $\times$ (cap. in op. + cap. in previous op.)

$$FOIP = 3 \times 3 + 2(2 + 3) + 1(1 + 2 + 3) = 25 \text{ hours}$$

With dispatch thus organised it makes no difference what order the capacities per operation are in. With one hour followed by three and then two hours we have:

$$FIOP = \text{cap. in op.} \times (\text{cap. in op.} + \text{cap. in previous op.})$$
$$= 1 \times 1 + 3(3 + 1) + 2(2 + 3 + 1) = 25 \text{ hours}$$

and with two hours followed by three and then one hour:

$$FOIP = \text{cap. in op.} \times (\text{cap. in op.} + \text{cap. in previous op.})$$
$$= 2 \times 2 + 3(3 + 2) + 1(1 + 2 + 3) = 25 \text{ hours}$$

9.3 Efficiency of Capacity as a Function of Demand

Take for instance an item involving a four-hour, a two-hour and a one-hour operation, which can only sustain 100% performance by all concerned if the minimum of capacity employed on it is $4 + 2 + 1 = 7$, or else a multiple of that many operators. It follows that even the smallest of factories, with seven men working on an item which takes seven man-hours to make at the rate of seven units in as many hours, will have to sell these at the same rate. Production to match a slower offtake, for instance one sale every two hours, would require less than 100% performance by the factory. Formulated:

$$\eta = \frac{n_1 + n_2 + \ldots}{u(n_1/u + n_2/u + \ldots)}$$

where n_1, n_2, etc. are the hours per operation and u is the time in hours to sell one unit, whilst the fractions n_1/u, n_2/u and so on are deemed rounded to the next higher integer.

Example: An item is made in three operations taking four hours, two hours and one hour, respectively. The utmost efficiency attainable in the particular factory is

$$\eta = \frac{4+2+1}{2(4/2+2/2+1/2)} = \frac{7}{2(2+1+1)} = 7/8$$

Now, combining the second and third operations, despite extending the operation time from $2+1$ to four hours, would make the manpower efficiency:

$$\eta = \frac{4+4}{2(4/2+4/2)} = 8/8 = 1$$

Although four men are needed to keep pace with sales in both cases, the latter arrangement is cheaper thanks to a shorter throughput time and less work in progress. It also creates far more scope for increased turnover by reducing the minimum workforce from $4+2+1$, to $1+1$.

9.4 Effect of Number of Jobs on Batch Size

Factories making a wide range of items in small quantities for many different customers are prone to encounter extremely difficult technical problems, which they often try to solve by putting the products through many different processes one after another. Sometimes 10, and perhaps 20 or more jobs per item occur in factories where there may be 100 or more different kinds of operations in all. Hence the importance of knowing whether the range of jobs has much effect upon the batch size; after all, customers do not expect to have to wait (very much) longer than a year for their orders to be delivered. With this in mind we shall stipulate a delivery time of one year (figure 9.5). Where each item involves two jobs the

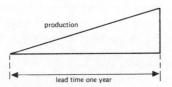

Figure 9.5   Batch size of one year throughput time and one job per factory order

total run will have to be split in two in order to make delivery in one year's time whilst maintaining 100% capacity utilisation (figure 9.6). And another split, this time into three parts, is needed to meet the same delivery date where each item involves three jobs (otherwise it would take three years, in all, to deliver one order). Cutting the delivery time from a year to six months would mean halving the batch size as well.

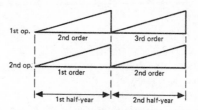

Figure 9.6   Batch size of one year throughput time and two jobs per factory order

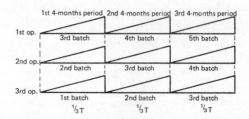

Figure 9.7   Batch size of one year throughput time and three jobs per factory order

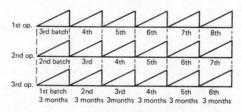

Figure 9.8   Batch size of 0.5 year throughput time and three jobs per factory order

In examples 9.4, 9.5 and 9.6, with delivery one year ahead, the numbers of batches a year can be calculated by means of the following formula:

$$S = \frac{b}{t} + b - 1 \text{ batches/year}$$

where b is the number of operations a year, S is the number of batches a year and t is the delivery time, in years.

Example 9.4

$$b = 1 \quad t = 1$$
$$S = 1 + 1 - 1 = 1 \text{ batch/year}$$

Example 9.5

$$b = 2 \quad t = 1$$
$$S = 2 + 2 - 1 = 3 \text{ batches/year}$$

Example 9.6

$$b = 3 \quad t = 1$$
$$S = 3 + 3 - 1 = 5 \text{ batches/year}$$

The formula must be altered where necessary to allow for delivery in less than (or more than) a year's time.

Example 9.7

$$b = 3 \quad t = 0.5$$
$$S = b/0.5 + b - 1 = 8 \text{ batches/year}$$

Example 9.8

$$b = 3 \quad t = 0.75$$
$$S = b/0.75 + b - 1 = 6 \text{ batches/year}$$

Where custom requires a forecast or statement of the total series it is as well to remember that for instance a total of 100 000 to be delivered in a year means only one order in progress throughout the year as one job per factory order (figure 9.5), whereas annual forecasts for the same total series will have to show three orders for 50 000 units apiece with two jobs per factory order (figure 9.7), and three orders for 33 333 units, or 166 665 in all, with three jobs per factory order involved (figure 9.7).

Given three jobs per factory order for delivery in six months' time, eight batches of 16 666 units will have to be included in the same annual forecast (figure 9.8). To calculate the number of batches with one year of delivery lead time ahead means taking double the number of jobs, less one.

$$S = 2b - 1$$

The batch size is the total series divided by the number of jobs, or $T = b \times S$.

9.5 Effect of Set-up Times on Number of Units Produced

The necessary set-up times, or set-up costs, are expressed in terms of their ratio v to the time per unit c, formulated $o = v \times c$. Example: $c = 5$ man-hours; set-up time 100 hours. Ratio v is then $100 \div 5 = 20$. The real annual output of a factory making one item in a single run supposedly of 100 000 units a year with $v = 100$ then becomes $100\,000 - 100 = 99\,900$ units per year. If produced in 10 batches a year the true annual output of the same item will be $10 \times (10\,000 - 100)$, or $100\,000 - 1000 = 99\,000$ units, adding 1% to the factory costs.

Given 100 orders instead the annual output would be $100(1000 - 100)$, or $100\,000 - 10\,000 = 90\,000$, that is 11% more in factory costs, whilst splitting the total series into 1000 batches would virtually halt production, since the 'output' would then be $1000 \times (100 - 100)$, or $100\,000 - 100\,000 = 0$.

Formulated, then, the effect of set-up time upon output is:

$$n = T - vs, \text{ in units per year}$$

where

> n is the real output of units a year
> T is the yearly output of an annual series without set-up costs
> s is the true number of batches a year
> v is the ratio of change-over time to time per unit.

9.5.1 Effect of number of batches upon indirect costs

Change-over costs are deemed to include all expenditure owing to the variety of work, in multiple-batch production and so on. Because much of the work of selling, methods engineering and draughting, planning, factory paperwork, invoicing and so forth in offices, as well as of retooling, set-up and other activities in factories contributes to change-over costs, these are prone to being surprisingly high. Moreover, indirect change-over costs increase with (but more steeply than) the number of batches a year. Figures (admittedly imaginary) are given in the following table, from which it will be evident that 'batching' should be avoided, or eliminated wherever possible, hence the importance of properly organised production.

Table 9.1

s	Indirect	Direct $v = 100$	Delivery $n = T - vs$	Payable $5 = T + 2$	Price factor $6 = 5/4$
1	2	3	4	$5 = T + 2$	$6 = 5/4$
0	0	100	100 000	100 000	1
1	100	100	99 900	100 100	1.002
10	1000	100	99 000	101 000	1.02
100	8000	100	90 000	108 000	1.20
800	40 000	100	20 000	140 000	7

9.6 Effect of Batch Size and Terms of Delivery on Spoilage Costs

9.6.1 Principles

A percentage defective must be established for each job. Spoilage per item is the sum of spoilages per job.

Example 9.9

Three per cent spoiled on the lathe, 2% on the milling, and 1% on the drilling machine means 6% defective in the factory order. To discover the consequences of spoilage upon an order we must allow for the following possibilities:

From one, to 20 jobs per item (many factories average three or four)

final inspection; interjob inspection is, at any rate, extremely
rare

customer will only accept exactly the number ordered, no more
and no less

customer willing to tolerate minor deviations from quantity
ordered

order too urgent to permit any risk of stock-out of certain
components.

How all this affects the cost price of production will now be explained
with the aid of some fairly realistic examples. Suppose:

Average batch size	10
Average spoilage per operation	2%
Average number of jobs	3

$$\frac{\text{Set-up time}}{\text{Cycle time}} = 15$$

u_p = material spoilage per item

u_{lk} = labour + costs of spoilage per item

Example 9.10

Batch inflation is ruled out. Rejects have to be remade. With 100
skilled men at a time working on as many of the aforementioned
batches, we have:

	Start	O.K. before operation	O.K. after operation
After first job, $100(S + 10c)$	1000	1000	980
After second job, $100(S + 10c)$	1000	980	960
After third job, $100(S + 10c)$	1000	960	940

Remake	Start	O.K. before operation	O.K. after operation
After first job, $60(S + c)$	60	60	60
After second job, $60(S + c)$	60	60	60
After third job, $60(S + c)$	60	60	60

Total made, $3 \times 100(S + 10c) + 3 \times 60(S + c)$

Chargeable, $3 \times 100(S + 10c)$

Labour + costs spoilage, $3 \times 60(S + c)$

In %, $u_{lk} = \dfrac{3 \times 60(S + c)}{3 \times 100(S + 10c)} \times 100 = \dfrac{60(15c + c)}{100(15c + 10c)} \times 100$

$$u_{lk} = \frac{60 \times 16}{100 \times 25} \times 100 = 38.4\%$$

Note: This maximum percentage is only attainable with spoilage spread over
as many batches as possible.

Example 9.11

Batch inflation ruled out, rejects need not be remade.

	Start	O.K. before operation	O.K. after operation
After first job, $100\,(S+10c)$	1000	1000	980
After second job, $100\,(S+10c)$	1000	980	960
After third job, $100\,(S+10c)$	1000	960	940

The next step is to calculate the percentage defective, depending upon the method of invoicing, according to one of the following two methods possible in principle:

Total manufactured, $3 \times 100\,(S+10c)$
Total chargeable, $3 \times 94\,(S+10c)$
Labour + costs of spoilage, $3 \times 100\,(S+10c) - 3 \times 94\,(S+10c) = 18\,(S+10c)$

$$\text{In \%,}\ u_{1k} = \frac{3 \times 6\,(S+10c)}{3 \times 94\,(S+10c)} \times 100 = \frac{6}{94} \times 100 = 6.4\%$$

Or

Total, $3 \times 100\,(S+10c)$
Total chargeable, $3 \times 100\,(S+9.4c)$
Labour + costs of spoilage, $3 \times 100(S+10c) - 3 \times 100(S+9.4c)$
$= 3 \times 100 \times 0.6c$

$$\text{In \%,}\ u_{1k} = \frac{3 \times 100 \times 0.6c}{3 \times 100\,(S+9.4c)} \times 100 = \frac{0.6}{15+9.4} \times 100 = 2.5\%$$

Example 9.12

Batch inflation employed, delivery must comply exactly with quantity ordered.

	Start	O.K. before operation	O.K. after operation
After first job, $100\,(S+10c+c)$	1100	1100	1078
After second job, $100\,(S+10c+c)$	1100	1078	1056
After third job, $100\,(S+10c+c)$	1100	1056	1037
Total work done, $3 \times 100\,(S+10c+c)$			
Total chargeable, $3 \times 100\,(S+10c)$			
Labour + costs of spoilage, $3 \times 100 \times c$			

$$\text{In \%,}\ u_{1k} = \frac{3 \times 100 \times c}{3 \times 100\,(S+10c)} \times 100 = \frac{c}{1+10c} \times 100 = \frac{1}{15+10} \times 100 = 4\%$$

Material spoilage has now become 10%.

Example 9.13

Batch inflation is employed and minor deviations from exact quantity ordered are tolerated. Calculated percentage defective again depends upon what is invoiced.

	Start	O.K. before operation	O.K. after operation
After first job, $100\,(S + 10c + c)$	1100	1100	1078
After second job, $100\,(S + 10c + c)$	1100	1078	1056
After third job, $100\,(S + 10c + c)$	1100	1056	1034

Total work done, $3 \times 100\,(S + 10c + 1c)$
Total chargeable, $3 \times 100S + 3 \times 1034c$
Labour + costs of spoilage, $3 \times 100S + 3 \times 1100c - 3 \times 100S + 3 \times 1034c$
$= 198c$

In %, $u_{lk} = \dfrac{198c}{300S + 3102c} \times 100 = \dfrac{198c}{4500c + 3102c} \times 100 = 2.6\%$

Or

Total work done, $3 \times 100\,(S + 10c + c)$
Total chargeable, $3 \times 100 + 3 \times 103.4S + 3 \times 1034c$
Labour + costs of spoilage, $300S + 3300c - 310.2S - 3102c = 198c - 10.2S$

In %, $u_{lk} = \dfrac{198c - 10.2S}{3 \times 103.4S + 3 \times 1034c} \times 100 = 0.6\%$

Or

Total work done, $3 \times 100\,(S + 10c + c)$
Total chargeable, $3 \times 100\,(S + 10c)$
Labour + costs of spoilage, $3 \times 100 \times c$

In %, $u_{lk} = \dfrac{300c}{300\,(S + 10c)} \times 100 = \dfrac{c}{S + 10c} \times 100 = \dfrac{1}{25} \times 100 = 4\%$

On average the customer then receives 10.34 units and pays for 10 of these.

9.6.2 The examples in a nutshell

	Material spoilage (%)	Labour + costs of spoilage (%)
No batch inflation, rejects remade	6	38.4
No batch inflation, rejects not remade	6	2.5, 6.4 Depending on method of invoicing

With batch inflation, keeping exactly to quantity ordered	10	4
With batch inflation, not keeping exactly to quantity ordered	6	2.6
		0.6
		4

Depending on method
of invoicing

The omission of batch inflation and remade rejects, as in the first example, is common in the case of large machines made one at a time or in batches of up to six. The planner should be well aware of the consequences his decision—for or against batch inflation—is likely to have on the ultimate price and delivery time (in fact almost all service orders necessitate such inflation coupled with tolerances on the order quantity). The most obvious solution is to match the quantity invoiced to that delivered, whilst allowing enough for set-up time per unit to be able to employ the formula:

$$(v/n + 1) \times \text{cycle time} \times \text{price per hour}$$

9.7 Effect of Throughput Time on Work in Progress

9.7.1 A specific example

Imagine a large engineering works complete with production bureau, purchasing department, foundry, pattern shop, job shop and assembly bay all involved in the manufacture of sizeable articles and operating independently under their own managers. The throughput times of the different departments coming after the production bureau are three, five, seven, four and six months, respectively. On average the production bureau takes a month to get going, after which the activities of the purchasing department, foundry and pattern shop proceed more or less concurrently, with the job shop and assembly bay bringing up the rear. The throughput time schedule is then as shown in figure 9.9.

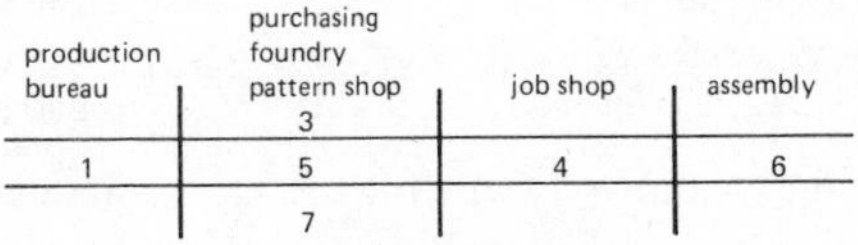

production bureau	purchasing foundry pattern shop 3	job shop	assembly
1	5	4	6
	7		

Figure 9.9

With seven months of throughput time imposed on all departments, capacity would be utilised as follows:

Production bureau	$1/7 = 14\%$
Purchasing	$3/7 = 44\%$
Foundry	$5/7 = 71\%$
Pattern shop	$7/7 = 100\%$
Job shop	$4/7 = 63\%$
Assembly bay	$6/7 = 86\%$

Yet factory policy is such that no manager would dream of allowing his department to operate at anything less than full capacity. Hence our first task is to seek a theoretical strategy consistent with 100% loading, which means using a TT = LCM (see section 9.2), with the following consequences (100% loading):

$$TT = LCM = 1 \times 3 \times 5 \times 7 \times 2 \times 2 \qquad = 420 \text{ months}$$
$$TTT \text{ (Total TT)} = LCM \times n = 420 \times 4 = 1680 \text{ months}$$
$$\text{Orders in progress} = LCM \qquad = 420 \text{ orders/TT}$$
$$\text{Total number of orders } LCM \times n \qquad = 1680 \text{ orders (without overlap)}$$

Once again it is fortunate that the TT need not necessarily equal the LCM to make 100% capacity utilisation possible. An optimum TT for this ratio of operation throughput times would be very difficult to establish and no factory thus organised would stand a chance of achieving such complete efficiency. For that matter no customer would tolerate the lead times involved. So let us see what can be done about the throughput times. For instance, could the pattern shop give priority to castings which have to go to the job shop, and arrange for the remainder to go direct to assembly whilst the job shop is doing that work? With this in mind we extend the pattern shop throughput time from seven, to ten months, whereupon the schedule becomes:

```
      | 3 |
  1 | 5 | 4 | 6
      | 10 |
```

Hence we have (with 100% loading)

$$TT = LCM = 1 \times 3 \times 5 \times 2 \times 2 \qquad = 60 \text{ months}$$
$$TTT = LCM \times n = 60 \times 4 \qquad = 240 \text{ months}$$
$$\text{Orders in progress} = LCM \qquad = 60 \text{ orders/TT}$$
$$\text{Total number of orders on hand} = LCM \times n = 240 \text{ orders}$$

This is a substantial improvement on the first schedule. But perhaps we can do still better by stepping up assembly so as to cut its throughput time from six, to five months.

```
    | 3 |
1 | 5 | 4 | 5
    | 10 |
```

Accordingly (again with 100% loading):

TT=LCM=$1 \times 3 \times 5 \times 2 \times 2$	= 60 months
TTT=LCM $\times n = 60 \times 4$	= 240 months
Orders in progress=LCM	= 60 orders/TT
Total number of orders on hand=LCM $\times n$	= 240 orders

Contrary to expectation, this makes no difference whatever. So we will try something else instead. What about extending purchasing throughput time from three, to five months (if need be by storing articles for two months)? Enquiries reveal that the job shop has been putting work out to contract which it could have done itself. We therefore increase its load by one month's work in four. The new schedule becomes:

```
    | 5 |
1 | 5 | 5 | 5
    | 10 |
```

which leads to:

TT=LCM	= 10 months
TTT=LCM $\times n = 10 \times$ TT	= 40 months
Orders in progress per TT=LCM	= 10 orders per TT
Total orders on hand LCM $\times n$	= 40 orders

This is a vast improvement. And now a very difficult task. The production bureau is asked to synchronise its activities with the initial production processes so as to in effect eliminate them from the schedule, whilst doubling the capacity and reducing throughput time in the pattern shop to five months. This is accomplished because everyone is aware of the need for it. Final schedule:

```
5 |
5 | 5 | 5
5 |
```

TT=LCM=5	= 5 months/TT
TTT=LCM $\times n = 5 \times 3$	= 15 months
Orders in progress TT $= \dfrac{\text{LCM}}{\text{HCF}} = \dfrac{5}{5}$	= 1 order per TT
Total orders on hand 1×3	= 3 orders

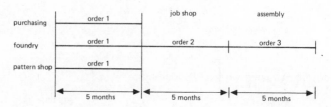

Figure 9.10   **Five departments fully utilised by three clients' orders**

We must conclude from this numerical example that strict allocation of capacity is less important than a stipulated *mandatory* throughput time for each department, or in other words that capacity should be organised flexibly enough to maintain the same throughput time throughout the production run for large orders of this kind. *A factory and its suppliers operate as a unit and should therefore seek the utmost efficiency by employing the same throughput times, in offices as well as in workshops (see also section 1.2).*

9.8 What Happens to Lead Time When the Factory is Fully Loaded?

Suppose that managerial policy is to insist upon 100% capacity utilisation, so that this one idea pervades the whole factory and everyone is so convinced of its merit that budgets and rating system are based on full loading as a matter of course. To determine the true state of affairs let us study the production figures for recent years, since it happens that the factory has been careful to keep exact records of all orders, decisions and post-calculations. We begin our study at a time when the workshop was equipped with three (identical) lathes, two (identical) milling machines and a drilling machine, whilst the order book contained 10 orders from as many different customers and involving 100 drawings each, or 1000 in all. Altogether these orders constituted 9000 hours of work, made up of 4000 hours of turning, 3000 of milling and 2000 on the drilling machine (thus averaging four hours of turning, three of milling and two of drilling for each of the drawings involved). In other words there was enough work to keep the factory going for $9000/(3 + 2 + 1) = 1500$ calendar hours.

Because the work had not been estimated at that time, no one was yet aware that the job ratio was $4:3:2$ and therefore inconsistent with the machine ratio of $3:2:1$. Our study reveals that the next 1300 calendar hours were to be spent as shown in table 9.2. In the

Table 9.2

Machine ratio	Op. 1	Op. 2	Op. 3
Start, backlog of work (hours)	4000	3000	2000
Completed after 1300 hours	$1300 \times 3 = 3900$	$1300 \times 2 = 2600$	$1300 \times 1 = 1300$
Still to be done	100	400	700

meantime more work, scheduled in the same ratio of job hours, has been accepted from the same 10 customers. Because 100 hours on operation 1 was less than a full week's work for three lathes, the new orders had already gone into production despite the substantial balance of earlier orders still outstanding (for instance 400 hours of milling, to say nothing of the 700 hours of drilling still to be done). Naturally, the customers were distinctly displeased at the consequent failure to meet delivery dates, and minutes of meetings held at the time suggest that the management were painfully aware of this. Efforts to complete delivery as quickly as possible were mainly concentrated on the third operation, as evidenced by the decision to buy another drilling machine, which altered the capacity ratio from $3:2:1$, to $3:2:2$.

Now that we know how the job ratio stood in relation to the machine ratio, and have analysed the orders, the remedy adopted seems logical enough at first sight. After all $1300 \times (3 + 2 + 1) = 7800$ of the total of 9000 hours work, or 87% of this, was completed in 1300 hours. But how much was actually delivered? Well, the backlog of 700 hours on the third operation was linked with one of $3/2 \times 700 = 1050$ hours on the second, and another of $4/2 \times 700 = 1400$ hours on the first operation, making $700 + 1050 + 1400 = 3150$ hours in all, the equivalent of $3150/9 = 350$ drawings. Now these were evenly distributed amongst the different orders with the result, as it later turned out, that no deliveries at all could be made.

The drilling machine had been supplied from stock and put into production immediately, thus creating the situation shown in table 9.3.

The purchase of the new machine was a source of satisfaction on the part of customers at the prospect of orders being delivered promptly one after another, and to the sales department, which had not yet realised that it would be expected to find more orders in consequence. In fact it seemed—at the time—that the increased capacity would not call for any more than the existing annual volume of orders (capacity in demand), although the works management did suspect that the second operation might now present something of a problem and therefore obtained the directors' consent to buy another milling machine. This came into operation after 600 calendar hours, enabling an extra 700 hours of work to be completed in the second period (of 1300 calendar hours). The initial situation is shown in table 9.4, and that after delivery of the third milling machine in table 9.5.

History then repeated itself in that the same customers ordered similar work with the same lead time (table 9.6). Investigation after 1300 hours would then have revealed waiting time and underloading in operations 2 and 3. The time spent on operation 1 is $1300 \times 3 = 3900$ hours. That is possible. The time spent on operation 2 is $1300 \times 3 = 3900$ hours, with only 3100 hours of work to be done. The

Table 9.3

	Op. 1	Op. 2	Op. 3
Backlog of original orders (hours)	100	400	700
Extra hours for new orders	4000	3000	2000
Total backlog (hours)	4100	3400	2700

Table 9.4

Machine ratio 3:2:2	Op. 1	Op. 2	Op. 3
Backlog (hours)	4100	3400	2700
Completed after 600 hours	$600 \times 3 = 1800$	$600 \times 2 = 1200$	$600 \times 2 = 1200$
Balance (hours)	2300	2200	1500

time spent on operation 3 is $1300 \times 2 = 2600$ hours, with only 2100 hours of work to be done.

A mere 1000 calendar hours of this was bound to create a critical situation, with the management crying out for orders and continually booking waiting hours, yet making no deliveries whatever. The situation is summarised in table 9.7.

It will be evident that 3000 hours spent on the first operation means not more than $3/4 \times 3000 = 2250$ hours of work on the second, and a mere $2/4 \times 3000 = 1500$ hours on the third operation (job ratio $4 : 3 : 2$). And that brought our study up to date.

Table 9.5

Machine ratio $3:3:2$	Op. 1	Op. 2	Op. 3
Backlog (hours)	2300	2200	1500
Completed after 700 hours	$700 \times 3 = 2100$	$700 \times 3 = 2100$	$700 \times 2 = 1400$
Balance (hours)	200	100	100

Table 9.6

Machine ratio $3:3:2$	Op. 1	Op. 2	Op. 3
Backlog (hours)	200	100	100
Hours for new orders	4000	3000	2000
Total backlog (hours)	4200	3100	2100

Table 9.7

Machine ratio $3:3:2$	Op. 1	Op. 2	Op. 3
Backlog (hours)	4200	3100	2100
Work done in 1000 calendar hours	$1000 \times 3 = 3000$	$1000 \times 3 = 3000$	$1000 \times 2 = 2000$
Not yet done (hours)	1200	100	100

Critical re-examination of the data revealed the surprising fact that full loading had been sustained (officially at any rate) for no less than 4300 calendar hours, something which could only have been accomplished by continually tailoring the orders to suit the machine ratio, or in other words by selecting jobs time after time in the ratio of $3:2:1$ (initially, and later in those of $3:2:2$ and $3:3:2$). We could only assume that elements of new orders had been dispatched well before they were due, whenever it became impossible to obtain jobs in the proper ratio from the orders then in progress. Proof of this is not too difficult to find, it being self-evident that:

(1) Four hours of work on operation 1 makes three hours available for operation 2 and two hours for operation 3 (order ratio $4:3:2$).
(2) The machines cannot handle any more than their maximum capacity.

Now, $1300 \times 3 = 3900$ hours of work completed on the first operation in 1300 calendar hours give scope for $3/4 \times 3900 = 2925$ hours on the second, but only 2600 hours of capacity are available for this, leaving 325 hours of work undone. Similarly, the 2600 hours spent on the second, give scope for two-thirds of that time, or 1733 hours on the third operation, for which only 1300 hours of capacity are available, leaving 433 hours of work undone. To sum up:

After 1300 hours:

> 3900 hours of work done on operation 1.
> 2600 hours of work done on operation 2, leaving 325 hours of work undone.
> 1300 hours of work done on operation 3, leaving 433 hours of work undone.

And after the second period of 1300 hours (with a second drilling machine in operation):

> Another 3900 hours of work done on operation 1.
> Another 2600 hours of work done on operation 2, leaving twice 325, or 650 hours of work undone.

Operation 3 has made up its backlog of 433 hours plus 1733 of the hours of work created by operation 2, or 2166 hours in all, but had enough capacity for 2600 hours.

Calculation shows that this means that operation 3 would have been underloaded after $1300 + 650 = 1950$ calendar hours, unless new orders were started at that time, in which case the other job ratios must have grown steadily worse. Our presence at the last meeting held to discuss delivery times happened to coincide with a visit by the directors of one of the factories supplied, who called to enquire about deliveries and the prospect of meeting delivery dates and were assured that this would be done in future at all costs. We shall now see how expensive a promise that proved to be.

9.9 Cost of Meeting Delivery Dates 'at all costs'

Some months later we find the factory faced with a backlog of 4000 hours' work, spread over 400 drawings, that is an average of 10 hours per drawing, including five hours of turning, three of milling and two on the drilling machine. At least the exact times are now known, since the work has been estimated, and that the total ratio is prone to vary around the $3:2:1$ mark. Moreover the total capacity requirement is known to be in the region of 12 000 hours a year and with that in view the factory is equipped with three lathes, two milling machines and one drilling machine. Factory policy is now based on two principles:

(1) No item can be delivered promptly unless all its parts are completed on time.
(2) Operations must begin, and end in unison, or in other words identical throughput times and simultaneous transfer are deemed essential.

The order book is produced and planning begins. Throughput times of 5, 6, 7, 8, 10 and 12 hours are tried first with a view to matching the factory load factor (job ratio $5:3:2$; capacity ratio $3:2:1$).

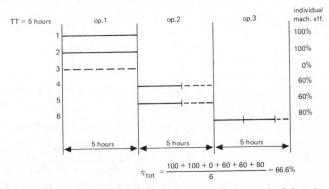

$$\eta_{tot} = \frac{100 + 100 + 0 + 60 + 60 + 80}{6} = 66.6\%$$

Figure 9.11 Fixed throughput time per operation of five hours

Although jobs could be progressed three at a time (see figures 9.11–9.16) through the first operation, there is no point in doing so when the second and third operations cannot cope with more than two apiece in the five hours available. Operation times per job must not cut across the (vertical) time line. Horizontally, capacity expended, available and in demand is represented by solid lines, with vertical dashes to mark the duration of each job. The dotted lines denote unused capacity. Throughput times of 6, 10 and 12 hours produce the best results. Of course we also try the 'theoretical' optimum throughput time as calculated from the LCM of the job

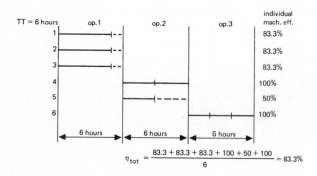

$$\eta_{tot} = \frac{83.3 + 83.3 + 83.3 + 100 + 50 + 100}{6} = 83.3\%$$

Figure 9.12   Fixed throughput time per operation of six hours

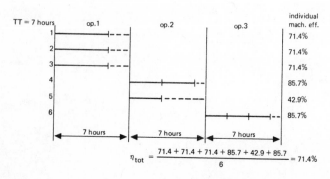

$$\eta_{tot} = \frac{71.4 + 71.4 + 71.4 + 85.7 + 42.9 + 85.7}{6} = 71.4\%$$

Figure 9.13   Fixed throughput time per operation of seven hours

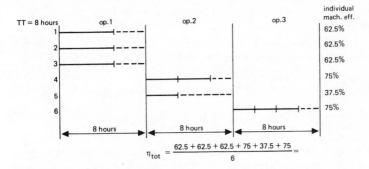

$$\eta_{tot} = \frac{62.5 + 62.5 + 62.5 + 75 + 37.5 + 75}{6} =$$

Figure 9.14   Fixed throughput time per operation of eight hours

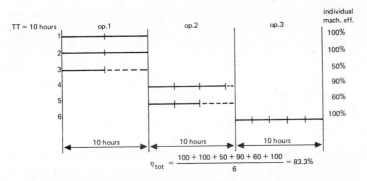

$$\eta_{tot} = \frac{100 + 100 + 50 + 90 + 60 + 100}{6} = 83.3\%$$

Figure 9.15   Fixed throughput time per operation of 10 hours

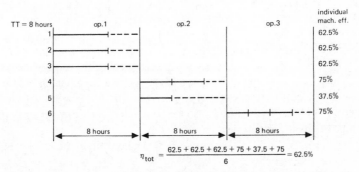

$$\eta_{tot} = \frac{62.5 + 62.5 + 62.5 + 75 + 37.5 + 75}{6} = 62.5\%$$

Figure 9.16   Fixed throughput time per operation of 12 hours

ratios (LCM = $5 \times 3 \times 2 = 30$ hours). The output of 30 hours' production is:

First operation: $30/5 \times 3 = 18$ units
Second operation: $30/3 \times 2 = 20$ units
Third operation: $30/2 \times 1 = 15$ units

Because the 15-unit output of operation 3 sets the pace, the efficiency is:

$$n = \frac{100 + 100 + 50 + 100 + 50 + 100}{6} = 83.3\%$$

Therefore this makes absolutely no difference as compared with the shorter throughput times of 6, 10 and 12 hours. The policy of prompt delivery 'at all costs' would involve a load factor of 83.3% (although it is debatable whether 'in fact' this is any less than the allegedly 100% work load dictated by the original policy).

Before introducing simple formulae with which to correct the aforementioned underload, let us consider another relevant example. Work (each unit) on the order book involves five hours of turning, four of milling and three of drilling, to be done on five lathes, four milling machines and three drilling machines available in the factory. That is of course ideal. The TT is $5 \times 4 \times 3 = 60$ hours and the TTT (total throughput time) $60 \times 3 = 180$ hours.

There are 180 units in progress, which is too many in view of the cost of materials; hence we are thinking in terms of another throughput time which would cut down the work in progress considerably, albeit with some loss of efficiency. A 15-hour throughput time creates the pattern of figure 9.17 (operations from top to bottom). The first and third operations permit 100% capacity utilisation, whilst the second completes 12 units in as many hours. Three operators on an hour's overtime and another on an authorised 3-hour standby will cost three hours of overtime and three hours of waiting time, against a saving of $180 - 45 = 135$ units in progress. Rejection of overtime would mean scheduling as shown in figures 9.18 and 9.19 (with 12 units in progress through each operation). It would seem more sensible to try 16 hours of throughput time, which indeed proves to result in far better loading than a TT of 15 hours without overtime. The efficiency can also be calculated with the aid of two simple formulae, as follows:

(1) With the LCM of job ratios as throughput time, the efficiency, or load factor is:

$$\eta = (M/W)_{min} \times \Sigma W / \Sigma M$$

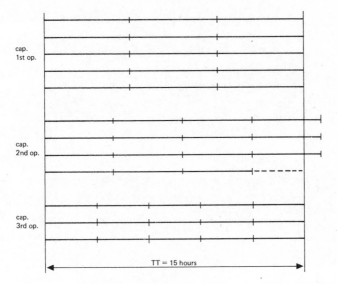

Figure 9.17 Fixed throughput time with a need for overtime

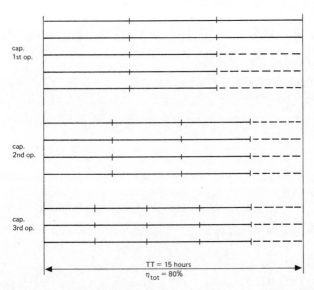

Figure 9.18 Fixed throughput time of 15 hours and 80% utilisation

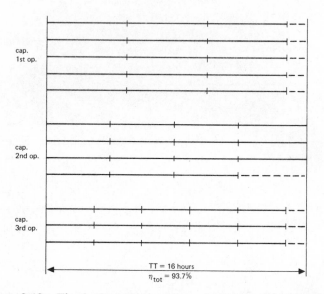

Figure 9.19 Fixed throughput time of 16 hours and 93.7% utilisation

where M is the machine capacity of the operations and W is the ratio of hours per job. For example, suppose the job ratio is $5:3:2$ and the machine capacity ratio $3:2:1$. Before applying the formula we must seek the smallest ratio of M to W, that is 3/5 in the first, 2/3 in the second, and 1/2 in the third operation. Therefore the last ratio is the minimum. The sum of magnitudes in the job ratio is $5+3+2=10$ and the sum of machines $3+2+1=6$. Thus,

$$\eta = 1/2 \times 10/6 = 10/12 = 83.3\%,$$

which agrees with the result obtained earlier.

(2) Where TT does not equal LCM the formula becomes:

$$\eta = p_{\min}/\text{TT} \times \Sigma W/\Sigma M$$

where M is the machine capacity, W is the number of process hours, $p_{\min}$ is the smallest quotient of TT/work (which should be rounded to the next lower integer). For example, with the same work as before, but with a TT of 8, the following p values are obtained:

1st op.: $8/5 \times 3 = 1 \times 3 = 3$
2nd op.: $8/3 \times 3 = 2 \times 2 = 4$
3rd op.: $8/2 \times 1 = 4 \times 1 = 4$

Therefore $p_{min} = 3$, and

$\eta = 3/8 \times 10/6 = 30/48 = 62.5\%$

This is the correct result. (See figure 9.14.)

Armed with these formulae we can now check the drawings mentioned at the beginning of this section.

Job ratio $5:3:2$ Machine ratio $3:2:1$

TT =	$p_{min} =$	$\eta(\%) =$
5	2	$2/5 \times 10/6 = 66.6$
6	3	$3/6 \times 10/6 = 83.3$
7	3	$3/7 \times 10/6 = 71.4$
8	3	$3/8 \times 10/6 = 62.5$
10	5	$5/10 \times 10/6 = 83.3$
12	6	$6/12 \times 10/6 = 83.3$

Everything tallies!

Now that we know the load factor to depend for the most part upon the smallest ratio M/W, we can easily calculate how best our factory could have been organised to make the most of its capacity hitherto. Remember that the job ratio was $5:3:2$ and the machine ratio $3:2:1$. With TT = LCM we have:

$$\eta = (M/W)_{min} \times \Sigma W/\Sigma M$$

where M/W is $3/5$ for the first operation, $2/3$ for the second operation, and $1/2$ for the third operation. The smallest (minimum) ratio is $1/2$ and the largest (maximum) $2/3$. What must be done to bring all three ratios to the maximum level?

1/2 becomes 2/3 when multiplied by 4/3
3/5 becomes 2/3 when multiplied by 10/9
$5:3:2 = 3x:2:1y$ thus becomes
$5:3:2 = 3 \times 10/9:2:1 \times 4/3$ or
$5:3:2 = 3\frac{1}{3}:2:4/3$

That being so, $(M/W)_{min}$ will be $2/3$ for all three operations, whilst the job ratio remains $5:3:2$ so that the sum of its magnitudes is still 10. The capacity ratio becomes $3\frac{1}{3}:2:4/3$, with a sum of magnitudes $6\frac{2}{3}$.

Verified by means of the formula

$$\eta = (M/W)_{\min} \times \Sigma W/\Sigma M$$
$$\eta = 2/3 \times 10 \times 3/20 = 100\%$$

Or in words, strict adherence to throughput times and therefore to delivery dates would have been possible given the facilities to increase output in the ratio of a third to three, or 11% during the first, and in the ratio of a third to one, or 33% during the third operation. Even supposing that there was or is no scope, or perhaps no need for increased production, it would still be possible to redistribute the workforce amongst the machines as follows:

$$5:3:2 = x:y:z, \text{ where } x+y+z = 6$$

Again a matter of simple arithmetic, producing the following result:

$$5:3:2 = 3:1\tfrac{4}{5}:1\tfrac{1}{5}, (M/W)_{\min} \text{ is now } 3/5 \text{ throughout}$$
$$\eta = 3/5 \times 10/6 = 100\%$$

Lastly an example based on the job and machine ratios stipulated in section 9.8. The job ratio is $4:3:2$, the machine ratio $3:2:1$.

$$\eta = (M/W)_{\min} \times \Sigma W/\Sigma M$$

$$\eta = 1/2 \times 9/6 = 9/12 = 75\%$$

Greater efficiency then calls for a $(M/W)_{\min}$ of 3/4 in all three operations where overtime, or subcontracting is to be the remedy, which therefore involves changing first 1/2 and then 2/3 into 3/4. Since $1/2 \times x/y = 3/4$, therefore $x/y = 6/4 = 1\tfrac{1}{2}$ and $2/3 \times x/y = 3/4$, and $x/y = 9/8$, that is for one machine, and since we have two of them $2 \times 9/8 = 2\tfrac{1}{4}$. The new ratios are then:

work $4:3:2$, machines $3:2\tfrac{1}{4}:1\tfrac{1}{2}$

Check:

$$\eta = 3/4 \times 9/6.75 = 100\%$$

If capacity in demand does not warrant the above remedy, a 100% efficiency can be obtained by 'switching' during part of the throughput time.

Retaining the median M/W ratio of 2/3, we then find that 3/4 changes to 2/3 as follows: $3/4 \times x/y = 2/3$ and $x/y = 8/9$ for three machines, reducing the work load of the first operation by $3 \times 1/9 = 1/3$ in all. $1/2 \times x/y = 2/3$ and $x/y = 4/3$ for one machine.

In other words the new job and machine ratios are $4:3:2$ and $2\frac{2}{3}:2:1\frac{1}{3}$, respectively. Check:

$$\eta = 2/3 \times 9/6 = 100\%.$$

In a factory, men and machines are around for a considerably longer period than client orders. In the course of time the 'technical contents' of the orders will change. Even if those changes are small and few in a given period of time, the effects on utilisation, throughput time and work-in-progress, as shown by the calculations in the examples, will nevertheless be considerable if those small changes have gone unnoticed and timely adaptive actions, using the calculations of this and the preceding chapter, have not been undertaken.

In a future publication the problems of order sequencing and job loading will be discussed. It will then become clear how the best planning system can be designed for every type of situation where such an effort can be meaningfully undertaken. Shortest possible and reliable delivery dates then become a reality.

Appendix

Planning Factors

That planning is a complex process will be evident from the multitude of factors it involves.

In the first place there are three distinct aspects of every incoming order to be considered, namely:

> The customer's order: whatever the customer orders and expects to receive and pay for as a single consignment.
>
> The factory order: whatever the factory produces and is paid for—at internal standard prices—as a single batch.
>
> The job: whatever fraction of a factory order is completed (usually) by one person at one work station (on a lathe, milling machine, etc.).

A full task comprises jobs together constituting so many hours' work, perhaps enough for a day or up to a week.

Jobs are transformed through 'operations' (with which they are often confused in common usage, a source of much misunderstanding).

Now, a factory order may be equivalent to, smaller, or larger than the customer's order in terms of drawings involved and units to be produced. Moreover it may, or may not be identical with another, earlier factory order and may go into continuous, or intermittent production as one job, or several in a fixed, or indeterminate sequence of operations.

Each factory order may, or may not involve as many jobs as any other. Note also that as many individual items in production are troublesome as plain sailing, whilst set-up time and/or time per unit may, or may not vary substantially from job to job. It may happen that special tools are needed, in which case these may have to be made before production begins.

Dispatch may involve individual 'time horizons', perhaps at, within, or beyond the limit to which full loading can be sustained, and is just as likely to be with, as without overlap. Another uncertain aspect is performance in terms of speed and spoilage, which varies from one operator to the next.

The chances that 100% loading will have to be achieved, as a matter of urgency, after one, or every other factory order at a time, or within some stated period such as a day, two days, a week, a month, or two months are likewise even.

Again, regular customers may, or may not have to be served exactly on time, whilst customer's orders are just as prone to be consistent, as inconsistent in terms of frequency and quantity ordered. Some goods can, and others cannot be delivered from stock, just as some customers are, and others are not prepared to accept anything other than the exact quantity ordered.

Orders from new customers may happen to coincide with periods of steady, increasing, or falling demand and then either trickle in slowly enough to be coped with adequately, or come in such a rush that emergency measures (sub-contracting, or turning customers away) are unavoidable. Hence new customers are not always welcomed with open arms. A limited number of basic materials may have to be ordered in large quantities, or a wide range of them a few at a time. Last, but by no means least, these materials may be expensive, or less so and have either long, or short lead times.

Index

Added value   12
Assembly   63
Authoritarianism   19

Batch sizes   8, 15, 22, 79, 95,
     120
   inflation   100
Block diagram   22–5

Capacity   28–30, 88–9
   available   27–8, 35, 45,
        51–2
   efficiency   94, 104
   in demand   27–8, 45, 51–2
   minimum   34, 89, 91
   underloading   56
   utilisation   12, 28, 34, 36, 39,
        72, 111
      100%   28, 34, 106–7
Cooperation   19
Cost
   indirect   99
   price   8, 100
   production   3, 12
   spoilage   99
   stock   15
Customer   4, 8, 10, 13–14, 22,
        80, 88, 120–1
Cycle time   79

Day's usage   5–9
Day's work   45
Defective items: see Rejects
Delay   38, 80
Delegation   18

Delivery date   3, 84
Demand in number of days   5,
        9
Democracy   19
Dispatch   32–3, 42, 44, 46–7
   decision rules   21, 37, 66
Down-time   37, 68, 84

Earliest delivery date   38
Earliest scheduled start   38

Factory order   26–8, 120
First come, first served   37
Flow chart   24–5
Functions   22

Idle time: see Waiting time
Industrial relations   3
Information   18–20, 35,
        79–80, 84, 88
Instructions   20
Inventory: see Stock

Job   16, 27, 37, 120

Labour relations   56
Lead time: see Throughput time

Machine   9, 44, 79, 109–110
   load factor   7, 13
Management   19, 22, 80, 107
Material   4, 121
   procurement   84

Network   38, 61, 63

On-line computer systems   39
Operation time   27, 37–8, 47
Operations, sequence of   30,
　　39–40, 53, 61, 120
Operator   43, 78, 84
Orders
　additional   4, 10–11
　administrator   80
　book   88
　increase   3, 10
　intervals   3, 5, 7
　quantity   5, 9, 84
　repeat   16
Organisation   79
Overhaul   84
Overlap   33, 42, 44, 50, 55–6

Performance   35, 88
Planning factors   120
Price factor   12
Process time: *see* Operations
　　time
Product group   44, 89–91
Products   4
Productions
　continuous   4, 120
　discontinuous   4, 120
Productivity   3, 22, 36

Ratio
　of capacity per
　　　operation   46–9, 90–1,
　　　107
　of completion   90
　of product time and usage
　　　time   7, 75
Rejects   79–80, 103, 121
Relationships   20–1, 60

Rule 80–20   75

Scheduling
　heuristic   36–7
　quantum   36
　theatre-booking   16
Sequence
　of jobs: *see* Job
　of operations: *see* Operation
Set-up time   7, 9, 37, 63, 79, 98
Spoilage: *see* Rejects
Stock
　costs   15
　evaluations   13
　fluctuation   8
　level   7–8, 13, 41
　obsolescence   7, 12
　minimal   11
　peak level   9
Supplier   4, 8, 84, 88
Supply   10

Team-spirit   51
Throughput time   3–4, 27, 36,
　　40, 42, 44, 47, 51, 56, 61,
　　84, 87, 90, 96, 103, 106
Tool   9, 37, 84
Transport time   5, 6, 51, 54–5,
　　57

Unscheduled hours   87

Waiting time   37–8, 47

Work in progress
　in factory orders   91, 93
　in hours   3, 56, 68, 89, 92,
　　　94, 103